HENRY HUDSON

HENRY HUDSON

Doomed Navigator and Explorer

ANTHONY DALTON

VICTORIA · VANCOUVER · CALGARY

Heritage House Publishing Company Ltd.
heritagehouse.ca

Library and Archives Canada Cataloguing in Publication
Dalton, Anthony, 1940-, author
Henry Hudson : doomed navigator and explorer / Anthony Dalton.

(Amazing stories)
Includes bibliographical references and index.
Issued in print and electronic formats.
ISBN 978-1-77203-023-5 (pbk.).—ISBN 978-1-77203-024-2 (html).—ISBN 978-1-77203-025-9 (pdf)

1. Hudson, Henry, –1611. 2. Northwest Passage--Discovery and exploration—British.
3. Canada—Discovery and exploration—British. 4. Explorers—Great Britain—Biography.
5. Explorers—Canada—Biography. I. Title. II. Series: Amazing stories (Victoria, B.C.)

FC3211.1.H8D35 2014 910.92 C2014-903465-2 C2014-903466-0

Edited by Karla Decker
Series editor: Leslie Kenny
Proofread by Vivian Sinclair
Cover photo: The Last Voyage of Henry Hudson. John Collier. Library and Archives Canada C-002061.

This book was produced using FSC®-certified, acid-free papers, processed chlorine free, and printed with vegetable-based inks.

Heritage House acknowledges the financial support for its publishing program from the Government of Canada through the Canada Book Fund (CBF), Canada Council for the Arts and the province of British Columbia through the British Columbia Arts Council and the Book Publishing Tax Credit.

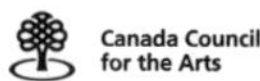

18 17 16 15 14 1 2 3 4 5
Printed in Canada

For
Lesley Reynolds,
my favourite editor,
with deepest appreciation

GREENLAND
Baffin Bay
Baffin Island
Arctic Circle
ICELAND
Reykjavik
Hudson Strait
Resolution Island
Hudson Bay
ATLANTIC
OCEAN
CANADA
James Bay
Akimiski Island
NOVA SCOTIA
UNITED STATES
OF AMERICA

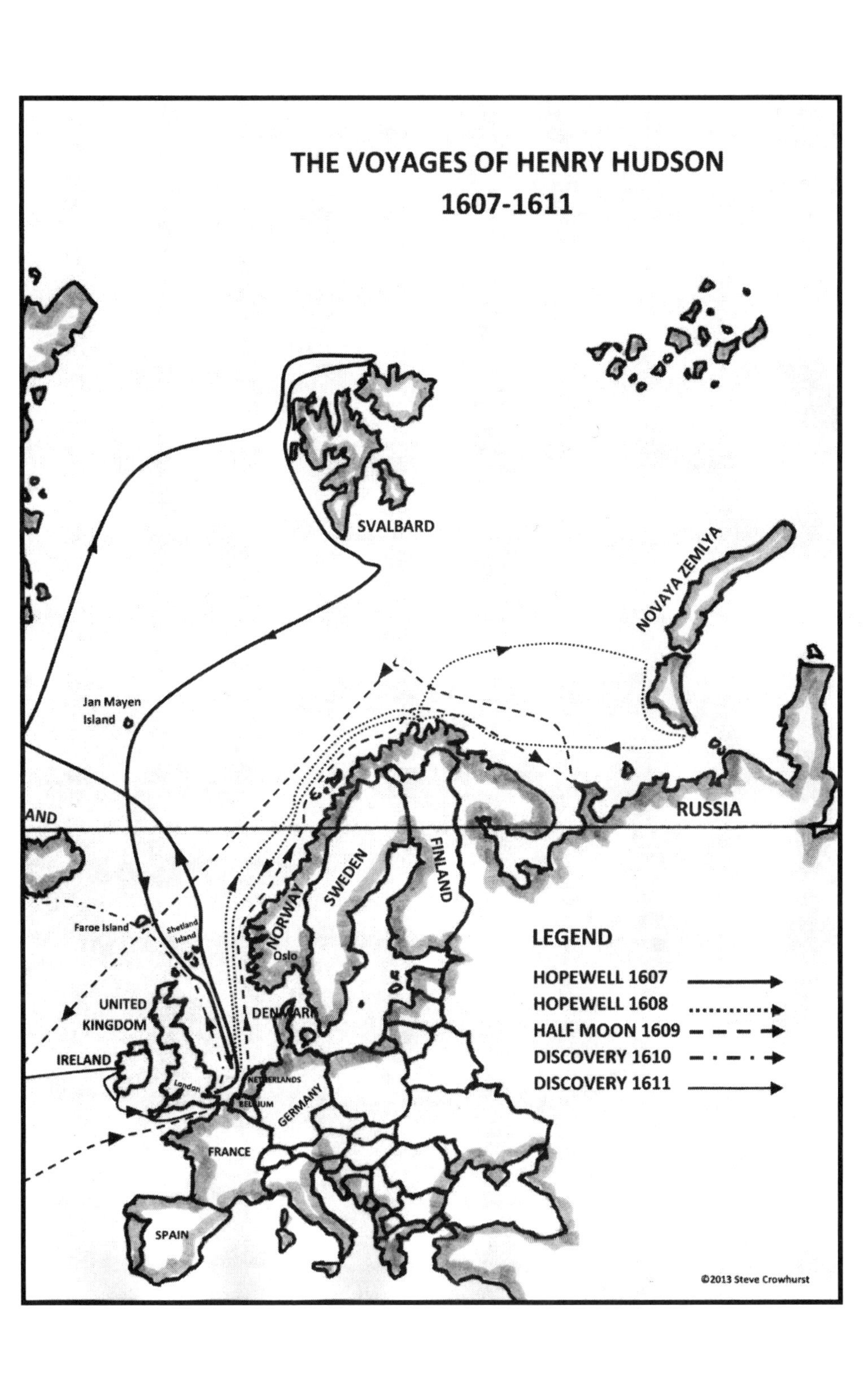

THE VOYAGES OF HENRY HUDSON
1607-1611
SVALBARD
NOVAYA ZEMLYA
Jan Mayen Island
RUSSIA
AND
FINLAND
SWEDEN
NORWAY
Oslo
Faroe Island
Shetland Island
UNITED KINGDOM
IRELAND
London
NETHERLANDS
BELGIUM
GERMANY
FRANCE
SPAIN
LEGEND
HOPEWELL 1607
HOPEWELL 1608
HALF MOON 1609
DISCOVERY 1610
DISCOVERY 1611
©2013 Steve Crowhurst

Contents

Although no true likeness of Henry Hudson is known to exist, this portrait is the most common representation of the seventeenth-century English explorer. LIBRARY AND ARCHIVES CANADA C-017727

Prologue

THE REMAINING NINETEEN MEN AND *two boys of* Discovery*'s crew were colder than they had ever been. Tired of spending every hour of each day and night in damp clothes, confined in a ship encrusted with ice inside and out, they were hungry, too, and had been for weeks—and they were so far from home. Many of them blamed the captain for their misfortunes. For months, their world had been this small sailing ship trapped in a frozen bay and a barren wilderness of white. The ptarmigan, geese, and other game that had kept them fed for the early winter of 1610–1611 had all but disappeared by the end of January. Within a few weeks, all that remained of the ship's rations was some bread and cheese.*

Captain Henry Hudson was suffering, too, but he held tight to his dream of finding a route through this icy land to the warmth and riches of Asia. Perhaps in an effort to raise the spirits of his crew, he distributed all the remaining bread among them. Most of them devoured their portions quickly, without thought for the days to follow. Occasional fishing expeditions helped somewhat, when the crew could find patches of open water, but there was never enough to fill their bellies for long.

Discovery *had sailed from England more than a year earlier. For many weeks the previous autumn, the ship had wandered back and forth across a large bay as the captain searched for a way out, convinced he was getting close to China. Then, when winter struck, they were beset by ice in a smaller bay to the southeast.*

By mid-June the ice had broken enough for Discovery *to be worked out of the bay and into the larger sea to the north. As the weather improved, the captain showed his determination to continue his search.*

The sailing was difficult and dangerous because of the big ice floes constantly moving around them. His eyes scanning the ice for avenues of open water, Hudson urged his unhappy crew on. One man sat high on the main mast, searching for a way out of the frozen maze. Others ranged along each side of the ship, armed with long poles to fend off the aggressive blocks of white and blue. Many of the crew worried they would be trapped in the ice for another winter.

Within a few days, the men were hungry again. Captain Hudson shared the last of the rounds of cheese among them. It was too little for most and, as it happened, too late for some. Talk of mutiny began to circulate among the crew.

Introduction

THE SEARCH FOR A NORTHWEST PASSAGE, a navigable waterway thought to extend across the top of North America, began in the late fifteenth century. At that time, British and European merchant enterprises were spending large sums of money and considerable time sending ships to Asia by way of the Cape of Good Hope at the southern tip of Africa. They believed there was a route over the top of the world, either over the North Pole or through one of two imagined ice-free water passages through the Arctic, a northwest or a northeast passage. The Arctic routes, if they existed, would be shorter by thousands of sea miles and were expected to reduce the length of the voyage by many weeks in each direction. The time saved would translate into lower transportation costs and therefore increased profits.

Before the dawn of the seventeenth century—not long before Henry Hudson's appearance on the polar exploration scene—around a dozen voyages to the Arctic had already been undertaken in search of a navigable route to the riches of the east—to China and the Spice Islands (now the Molucca Islands, part of Indonesia). These included two failed attempts by John Cabot (1497 and 1498), the first known expeditionary voyages to find a northwest passage. Sebastian Cabot, John's son, claimed to have entered what would become Hudson Straits in 1509, but he was not widely believed. Unknown Portuguese mariners certainly found their way into Hudson Bay during the mid- to late sixteenth century. They called it Baia dos Medaos (Bay of Medaos). Then there was Martin Frobisher. He made three voyages as far as southern Baffin Island in 1576, 1577, and 1578. The superb navigator John Davis explored the west coast of Greenland, the strait that now bears his name, and parts of eastern Baffin Island during three expeditions to find a northwest passage to Asia in 1585, 1586, and 1587. Many other voyages of north polar exploration would take place in the following five hundred years, none of which would prove successful. In fact, 409 years would pass between John Cabot's 1496 expedition and the eventual successful navigation of the Northwest Passage by Norwegian polar explorer Roald Amundsen, who made the voyage from 1903 to 1906.

The Northeast Passage was conquered somewhat earlier: Swedish explorer Baron Adolf Erik Nordenskiöld travelled it in 1878–1879 aboard the steam-powered ship *Vega*.

Gravesend, on the south side of the Thames River and just over twenty-two miles east of the heart of London, features in all four of Henry Hudson's known voyages. The last port on England's great river before the North Sea, it was visited by most of the famed British explorers of the fifteenth through the twentieth centuries and by more than a handful of foreigners. Pocahontas, the Powhatan "Indian princess" from Virginia who is said to have saved the life of Captain John Smith (a contemporary of Henry Hudson), died on board a ship out on the Thames and is said to be buried at or near St. George's Church, close to the waterfront.

In Henry Hudson's era, navigation charts of the lands bordering the North Atlantic and Arctic Oceans were limited in scope and far from complete or correct in detail. Navigational aids were few and primitive; the sextant would not be invented for another 150 years, and a means of determining exact longitude would not be discovered before the 1770s. The now ubiquitous Global Positioning System (GPS) was a technology of the distant future.

Ice was a serious problem for any ship venturing into Subarctic and Arctic seas. In the nomenclature of the North, there are bergy bits, floes, growlers, icebergs, and a handful of other names for broken ice. Bergy bits are usually huge pieces of floating glacier ice, measuring anywhere from 100 to 300 square metres (110 to 328 square yards), with up to 5 metres (5.5 yards) showing above sea level: in effect, a flat field of ice. Floes are smaller, up to 20 metres (21 yards) across. Growlers, mostly smaller in overall size than bergy bits, sit low to the surface of the sea, rarely standing more than 1 metre (1.1 yards) in height and measuring up to 20 square metres (21 square yards) in area. And then there are icebergs. These monster blocks of glacial ice are calved from slow-moving glaciers, such as the steady stream that breaks away from the majestic Melville Glacier on the west coast of Greenland.

In the 1930s, Captain Thomas Smellie, master of the HBC steamship RMS *Nascopie,* reported steaming for a full hour past a monstrous iceberg in Davis Strait. He estimated it to be "a hundred feet high and ten miles long." In the sixteenth, seventeenth, and eighteenth centuries, polar mariners in small sailing ships with no survival equipment on board were in constant danger from marauding ice. This was the unpredictable white world into which Captain Henry Hudson took his small ships, his fellow officers, and his crews.

CHAPTER

1

Who Was Henry Hudson?

HISTORIANS HAVE CONSISTENTLY DRAWN A blank when searching for clues to the early life of English sea captain Henry Hudson. He is, without doubt, one of the most enigmatic figures in the history of seventeenth-century polar exploration.

Hudson is thought to have been born either in Hertfordshire or somewhere in Greater London around 1570; some say he may have been born much farther north, in Northumberland. The mystery remains unsolved.

What he looked like is also unknown. Although there have been a few paintings and sketches of the man, these images are false—nothing more than guesswork on the part of the artists. No accurate pictorial record exists.

The first historical knowledge of Henry Hudson dates to 1607, when he was already in his thirties. So what was his life like during his formative years, and what was he doing during his twenties? There are no answers, only conjecture and supposition.

Henry Hudson is thought to have been the son of a sea merchant. The family is believed to have had connections, through Henry's grandfather, to the London-based Muscovy Company, an established English trading consortium in whose service Henry Hudson is believed to have gone to sea while he was still a boy. It is possible that young Henry served for a while as a cabin boy or common seaman under the great navigator and North Atlantic veteran Captain John Davis. If he did so, that would account for his considerable knowledge of northern regions and his undeniable sailing and navigation skills. Davis made three voyages to what is now the Canadian Arctic between 1585 and 1588 and would have known something about the treacherous strait between Baffin Island and the mainland. If Henry Hudson sailed with him, he would have learned much from Davis about navigating in ice.

However he came by his skills, at the dawn of 1607 Henry Hudson was, by the standards of the day, an educated man. He could read and write. He had a working knowledge of mathematics. He could understand and follow directions on maps and nautical charts, he was an experienced sailor who had advanced to the rank of ship's captain, and he had a few influential friends. Those friends were important to Hudson because he was determined to make his name as an explorer. He needed to have a high profile to win future commissions.

Unfortunately, despite his status as a respected captain, Henry Hudson would prove to be devious in his dealings with his employers and would show that he was a poor judge of men. A captain was expected to stamp his authority on every aspect of his ship and his crews. In that, Henry Hudson was something of a failure. He often vacillated at sea, causing confusion among his officers and crews. He could be unnecessarily judgemental and often dangerously unfair in his decisions.

Away from the sea, Hudson appears to have been a happy family man, although obviously restless. He had a wife, three sons, and a granddaughter. Having a family, however, would not have prevented Hudson from accepting ocean-going commissions. It was not unusual in those days for seafarers to be away from home for many months at a time—sometimes a year or longer—with no communication from home for most, if not all, that time. Hudson's wife, Katherine, might not have liked it, but she would have understood.

Henry Hudson is believed to have married Katherine (there is no record of her last name) in the early 1590s. They lived in some comfort, for the times, in a three-storey brick house in London's St. Katherine's district, within walking distance of the Tower of London. The house would have been a narrow structure with small rooms, but it would have been far more comfortable than the accommodation owned or rented by most mariners. That the Hudson family was well off financially is suggested by the fact that they had a live-in maid to take care of the house and their three sons, Oliver, John, and Richard. Little is known of Oliver, other than that he was married and had at least one child, a daughter.

By the early eighteenth century, British and other European sailing ships had roamed much of the globe. They knew the extent of the world's oceans and the outlines of the continents. Spanish ships had been crossing the Atlantic to Central and South America for over two hundred years—and they had explored significant parts of the South Pacific. Portuguese ships had rounded southern Africa's Cape of Good Hope and crossed the Indian Ocean to trade with Asia. The Dutch had sailed and traded as far afield as modern-day Indonesia, and the British had left their national flag on the foreign soils of Africa, India, and North America.

What was missing from the nautical charts of the times was a clearly defined sea route across the top of the world—from Europe to Asia via a northeast or northwest passage, both of which would be icebound for most of each year.

Captain Henry Hudson, not yet a household name in England but building a reputation all the same in nautical circles, believed strongly in the existence of a northwest passage. He was also prepared to admit the possibility of a similar route to the northeast, across the northern shores of mighty Russia. If at all possible, he wanted to be the man to discover one or the other of these elusive northern passages.

CHAPTER

2

North Toward the Pole

COULD THERE POSSIBLY BE A navigable route to Asia over the North Pole? In the late sixteenth and early seventeenth centuries, that question was posed by European business leaders looking for a way to increase profits. They shared a fanciful notion that between the ice barrier and the Pole was open water for long distances. That tract of warmer water could, some believed, lead a ship on a shorter sea route from Europe to the riches of Asia—most importantly, China (or Cathay, as it was then commonly known).

In 1585, two English ships, *Sunshine* and *Moonshine*, left Dartmouth, Devon, on a combined fishing and exploration voyage toward the North Pole and, if possible, beyond to China. Financed by William Sanderson, a wealthy local fish merchant, the expedition was commanded by Captain John Davis, one of Queen Elizabeth's leading explorers. Davis did not get his ships anywhere near the Pole, but he did cross the North Atlantic Ocean and probe the Arctic waters between Greenland and Baffin Island—and made friends among the Native people of Greenland. He sailed far into what is now Cumberland Sound, some 180 miles, and convinced himself he had entered a northwest passage to China. Delighted with his finds, Davis hurried home to England to tell Sanderson of his discoveries, and of his cargo of products from a large number of seals and a whale or two.

Sanderson was pleased enough with Davis to send him back again the next year with an additional two ships, *North Star* and *Mermaid*. Davis, with *Moonshine* and *Mermaid*, returned to the ice-littered sea between west Greenland and Baffin Island. He sent the other two ships north from Cape Farewell on the southern coast of Greenland to explore its eastern coast. *North Star* and all its crew were lost, but the other three ships sailed on. Once again, Davis's ships failed to reach anywhere near the Pole, but he did return with three ships intact and hundreds of seal pelts stowed below decks, plus a cargo of cod.

John Davis went north again in 1587, sailing once more across the Atlantic to western Greenland. There, two ships left him for the cod-rich fishing grounds off Labrador while the expedition leader turned toward the Pole. Davis reached his farthest north at latitude 73° north, where Davis Strait opens into Baffin Bay, far short of latitude 90° at the top of the world. Stalled by headwinds, he could go no farther. On his way south, he crossed the wide mouth of an inlet where whirlpools and riptides tossed his ship around like a cork. Davis named it "The Furious Overfall." He didn't know it, but, like Martin Frobisher a decade before him, he had passed the wild strait that would one day be named after Henry Hudson. This third Arctic voyage was to be Davis's last to the northern regions. Part of his legacy was to perpetuate the myth, aided by the often relentless heat of the summer's midnight sun, that there might be a clear water route over the North Pole.

Twenty years later, as 1607 began, the money-hungry directors of the London-based Muscovy Company were planning an expedition of their own to attempt the North Pole route. Although they had the ships, and crews were easy to find in English seaports, they needed a captain with the necessary experience. To help them choose from the few qualified, available candidates, they turned to the seaport of Bristol, on the Severn River on England's west coast, to seek the advice of a respected man of great intellect.

Richard Hakluyt, a priest and a scholar, was known to be Britain's most knowledgeable source for information on exploration and the sea. In addition, Hakluyt knew many of the great British sea captains of the time. The Muscovy Company directors asked Hakluyt if he thought Henry

Hudson was the man for the job they had in mind. The two men were friends, and Hakluyt recommended Hudson without reservation. Hakluyt believed Hudson was the most qualified English explorer to lead a northern voyage of discovery. Most historians agree that Hudson's first major voyage of exploration as a captain was this one.

The directors of the Muscovy Company assigned their three-masted, square-rigged barque *Hopewell* to Hudson's North Pole expedition. Registered at about forty tons and probably no more than sixty feet long, *Hopewell* had been used in the company's Baltic trade for most of the three years since she was built. Inside her stout hull of good English oak was accommodation for the captain and eleven other men, one of whom was John Hudson, Henry's fourteen-year-old son. The rest of the space below decks would be filled with food and water supplies for the voyage.

Before embarking on the voyage in the third week of April 1607, Hudson, his officers, and crew took communion at St. Ethelburga's Church in Bishopsgate, London, a short walk from the river where the sailing ships were moored. The narrow church had seen London grow for three centuries by then. Hudson and *Hopewell*'s crew were just a handful of mariners among many who had prayed for a safe and successful voyage before St. Ethelburga's altar.

Their prayers said, Hudson and his crew followed the ancient streets, now growing damp with a thick mist coming off the Thames River. They boarded *Hopewell*, but a fog,

Captain Henry Hudson and his crew prayed in St. Ethelburga's Church in London before their attempt to reach the North Pole aboard *Hopewell*. GILLIAN BUTCHER

which would cause problems enough in the Arctic, now enveloped the ship, causing her crew to feel their way downriver, ship length by ship length. At Greenhithe, near Dartford, the fog closed in, making further progress impossible. For eleven days, Hudson and his crew were stalled at Greenhithe and later downriver at Gravesend, on the Thames estuary. The thick fog was followed by a violent storm blowing up the Thames from the North Sea. Those wasted days would have been frustrating in the extreme for Hudson, knowing as he did that the navigation season in the north was always short; every day counted. *Hopewell* finally departed from Gravesend on May 1, 1607. Once out of the wide estuary and into the North Sea, Hudson set a course for the Pole.

Although Captain Henry Hudson was the ship's master, another licensed captain was also on board. Captain William Collins had signed on as first mate and as such was second-in-command. Despite his experience and seagoing abilities, Collins's addition would not be as complementary to Hudson's team as it should have been. A clash between the two was not long in happening.

Hopewell's voyage north was slow; the winds were against the ship all the way. The log shows it took twenty-six days to sight the Shetland Islands and another week and a half to reach the Arctic Circle. The weather wasn't the only problem: all was not well on the ship. For reasons unknown, somewhere between Gravesend and the Shetlands, Hudson made drastic changes in the authority of three men on board. He demoted Captain Collins from mate to bosun. John Colman, a seaman, replaced Collins as mate. At the same time, James Young, the bosun, was demoted to common seaman. Hudson did not explain his actions in his log. However, Collins and Young, both experienced men, would have been highly insulted by Hudson's surprising actions. The seeds of discontent had been sown and would grow. Hudson should have known that a small sailing ship, particularly one in dangerous Arctic waters, was no place for disgruntled officers or crew; he risked so much by his inexplicable actions.

En route to the polar ice, the ship passed just east of the Shetland Islands and crossed the Arctic Circle well to the south and west of Bear Island. From there, Hudson appears to have deliberately ignored his orders to sail for the North Pole. Instead, *Hopewell* arced north and west to fetch the east coast of Greenland a few miles north of the immense coastal gash called Scoresby Sound, the longest fjord in the world.

Well aware that the directors of the Muscovy Company might not appreciate his lengthy detour, Hudson justified his actions by writing, "The chief cause that moved us thereunto, was our desire to see that part of Greenland, which (for ought that we know) was to any Christian unknown: and we thought it might as well have been open sea as land, and by that means our passage should have been the larger to the Pole . . . And considering we found Land contrary to that which our [navigation] cards make mention of; we accounted our labour so much the more worth."

The coast of Greenland was a depressing place for sailors confined in a tight space, especially an unhappy crew far from the comforts of home. The land was covered in white, and large ice floes littered the sea. Frequent dense fogs hampered navigation, and regular freezing rain squalls added to the misery (although none of that would have deterred Hudson). Working along the coast, *Hopewell* found a convenient sea current that eased her away from the dangers of the land and helped her on her way.

From the desolate eastern Greenland coast, *Hopewell* sailed north and east toward the polar ice pack. The immediate dangers from ice were behind the ship, but ahead, the crew's difficulties were about to resume. The farther north the ship sailed, the longer the daylight lasted. Soon there was little or no darkness at night: *Hopewell* had ventured into the land of the midnight sun. The sun shone for longer each day, when it could be seen, and the air became generally somewhat warmer. The balmier weather convinced Hudson that the theories of open water between the polar ice and the North Pole were correct. He looked forward to breaking through the ice barrier and enjoying smooth sailing at the top of the world, but it was a dream that would never be realized. The warmer summer weather did not stop the storms from battering *Hopewell.* Drifting ice also became a constant problem, often causing Hudson to change course to avoid its clutches.

In late June, *Hopewell* came in sight of the Spitsbergen

archipelago, also known then as New Land (*Nieuwe Land*), its original Dutch name. As the captain took his ship cautiously through the surrounding ice and between the islands, they were at constant risk. The coastlines were jagged rock covered with ice and snow. Testing the men to their limits, another vicious storm blew in without warning. While the storm raged—for a day and a night—all hands remained at work, some high in the rigging, the rest on deck. Captain Hudson spent the long, dangerous hours on the quarterdeck, issuing orders and using all his seamanship skills to keep his ship off the rocks and clear of the most dangerous ice. When the weather improved, Hudson continued north, following the land as it curved to the east. En route, he updated his charts, marking coastlines and distances. In this manner *Hopewell* sailed around the north coast of Spitsbergen.

Some of the crew killed a polar bear, and parts of it were cooked and served to the men. The meal was not a success. Hudson wrote, "Many of my company were sick with eating of a [polar] bear's flesh." They almost certainly made the mistake of eating the bear's liver. That organ in a polar bear is rich in vitamin A and extremely toxic to humans.

Ten weeks after leaving Gravesend, *Hopewell* approached a large bay on the northwest coast of North East Island, part of the Spitsbergen archipelago. Hudson wrote of the islands as "a very ragged land, rising like haycocks." (Centuries later, in 1974, British extreme sailor and polar mountaineer H.W. Tilman referred to Spitsbergen as "a wilderness of barren stones," yet that description, while accurate to a point, ignores the ice and snow that dominate the archipelago year round. It also ignores the abundant wildlife on the islands.)

On their difficult voyage across the Arctic Ocean from Greenland, Hudson and his crew had seen many whales, seals, and walruses—and more species of seabirds than most of them could count as they neared the islands. But nothing they had seen so far prepared them for what they saw in the bay: Hudson wrote the basics in his log but failed to capture the grandeur of the scene. He noted, "In this bay we saw many whales . . . " There were, in fact, hundreds of the leviathans all around the ship as she stood to her anchor. One came up under the ship and bumped the keel, scaring the crew but not causing any damage to the ship. (Three decades later, almost certainly as a result of Hudson's report of many whales in the region, the fjords on the north coast of Spitsbergen would be crowded with whaling ships.)

Hudson sent a small party of sailors ashore on North East Island to reconnoitre. John Colman and William Collins were in charge of this excursion, and they returned after many hours ashore with tales of seeing freshwater streams, ducks and geese, and distinct tracks of other creatures, including mammals large and small, such as bears and foxes. And, they said, the island's climate was warm. The warmth, of course, was no more than a seasonal lull due to the long hours under the midnight sun.

Between Greenland and Spitsbergen, *Hopewell*'s crew saw many marine mammals, including seals. ANTHONY DALTON

Henry Hudson was a determined and courageous man. Convinced he was within reach of open water that would take him over the Pole, he turned *Hopewell* to the north and left Spitsbergen in his wake. He didn't get far. The brief summer warmth of Spitsbergen had been an illusion. The polar ice pack soon blocked *Hopewell*'s route, stopping the ship at latitude 80° 23' north. The fact that no European had ever reached so far north was small consolation to Hudson: his attempt to reach China by way of the North Pole had failed. Not a quitter, Hudson resolved to try again by another route. His crew was not thrilled when he announced his plans to sail down the west coast of Spitsbergen 's main island, around the southern extremity, and up the east coast to see if there was open water that way. At that point he noted in his log his view of the commercial value of the archipelago: "I think this land may be profitable to those that may adventure it."

All the way along the western coasts of the islands, *Hopewell* battled storm after storm and had frightening encounters with polar ice. When large ice floes move with the winds and currents, they roll and they spin, sometimes slowly, sometimes with sudden, unpredictable movements. Their directions often conflict. When that happens, chaos ensues. Giant floes raft up and over each other, creating pressure ridges many metres high—higher than the tallest masts. Two or more floes grinding together can close around a ship and crush it in minutes. One such event almost caused the loss of the ship. Disaster was averted when Hudson took charge of a rowboat and urged the rowers to tow the sailing ship away from the danger.

Keeping *Hopewell* free of ice and out of harm's way would have been a formidable task requiring superb seamanship and great courage. Hudson had both, and although he was firmly set on succeeding, his resolve had to end: there was no open-water route that season on either coast. Disappointed again but acknowledging at last (and for now) that there was no navigable sea route to China over the North Pole, he told his men they were going home. The crew was delighted.

All sailing ships in the Arctic were at extreme risk from concentrations of ice floes. ANTHONY DALTON

Most sea captains, then and now, command their ships with great strength of character, good or bad. For much of the time, Henry Hudson did the same. Occasionally, though, his character seemed to lose its strength and become uncertain and devious. As master of his vessel, Hudson could effectively do as he wished without fear of reprisal from his crew or the ship's owners. If he chose to change course, he could do so with impunity. As a courtesy, under normal circumstances he would discuss his plans with senior officers but would not necessarily be swayed by their concerns, if any. Unfortunately, Hudson sometimes stepped away from his dominant role as captain and became almost Machiavellian, while at the same time showing his weaknesses. Those unfortunate aspects of his character would surface more and more over the next few years, at sea and on land.

The north coast of Greenland was some twenty-five degrees of longitude due west of Spitsbergen. Hudson wrote that he had intended to attempt a passage along the north coast of Greenland and then down the western coast to Davis Strait before heading back to England across the North Atlantic. Given Hudson's obsession with finding a northwest passage to China, it is possible that he had planned to search to the west once he had rounded the northern Greenland coast. Indeed, it is equally possible that his long detour west to Greenland at the beginning of the voyage had signified his intention to attempt the massive island's northern coast and then sail west earlier in the voyage. As it turned out, the ice between the two land masses (Greenland and Spitsbergen) at that high latitude proved impenetrable, so Hudson had to change his plans. On July 27, with the icy wind blowing from the west, *Hopewell* turned her bow southeast toward England.

Shifting, freezing winds forced *Hopewell* to make constant course changes for the next three or four days until land was sighted again on July 31. That land, then known as Cheries Island and now called Bear Island, is about one-third of the distance from the southern tip of Spitsbergen to the closest point in Norway. From that island, the most direct course to London would have been south-southwest, and that is the course that Hudson's log says he followed. But it cannot be true, because en route from Cheries Island to England, he discovered an island where no land was expected. The ship had stumbled upon a previously unknown island that Hudson named Hudson's Touches. It had no obvious commercial value, but it was a new discovery to place on the navigation charts of the North Atlantic. That island, now known as Jan Mayen Island, is southwest—not south-southwest—of Cheries Island, a considerable difference. The two locations are separated by more than twenty-five degrees of longitude, whereas a direct route to the mouth of the Thames would have had *Hopewell* crossing only eighteen degrees of longitude.

Was Hudson's navigation so far wrong? Or was he again looking for a way past Greenland to reach Davis Strait and search for a northwest passage? History shows that given his experience and the tools available to him (compass rose, backstaff, log line, and sandglass), it is unlikely Hudson's navigation was so inaccurate. However, from the newly discovered Hudson's Touches, he did turn his ship toward home.

En route, she called briefly at the Faroes on August 15, and one month later *Hopewell* finally made her way up the Thames estuary, arriving at Tilbury, opposite Gravesend, on September 15.

Dutch sea captain Jan May visited Hudson's Touches

a few years later. Captain May renamed it Jan Mayen Island and claimed the small piece of barren real estate for Holland. Evidently, the island was not considered significant by the British, since they failed to object to the change of ownership. Since 1921, the volcanic Jan Mayen Island has been Norwegian territory, though uninhabited except for a small scientific research station.

Even though Hudson was unsuccessful, despite his best efforts, in crossing the Pole and reaching China, his voyage proved to be of great potential benefit to the Muscovy Company. The knowledge he brought back of whales, walruses, and seals at Spitsbergen—all valuable commodities—made his expedition a huge commercial success.

CHAPTER

3

The Second Arctic Voyage

HENRY AND HIS SON JOHN spent a few months at home in London over the following winter with Katherine and the two older boys. The city would have been damp and cold, but it was certainly far more pleasant for the two sailors than the harshness of the high Arctic. Hudson spent some of this time in England conferring with his friend Richard Hakluyt about possible navigable routes through the Arctic. On his own maps, Hakluyt showed Hudson what he knew of the routes taken by Willem Barentsz and other polar explorers.

Dutch navigator and explorer Willem Barentsz had sailed from Amsterdam at the end of May 1594 to seek a northeast passage to China through the ice at the top of Russia. It was the first of three voyages he made to the region, none of which succeeded in getting past the long, slender island barrier of the Russian islands of Novaya Zemlya. Barentsz did manage to work his ship considerably farther north than John Davis had done in the waters off Greenland in 1587. Barentsz reached latitude 80° north, at the time the farthest north any European had attained. On his two later expeditions, Barentsz again ventured into the ice off northern Novaya Zemlya, continuing to search, without success, for a way past the remote island group. The third time he was especially unlucky: his ship was crushed by the drifting floes, and he and his men were forced to spend the winter in a hut they built on the shore. Barentsz and four of his crew died the following spring while attempting to reach the southern tip of Novaya Zemlya. Twelve other crew members survived and were rescued by Russian fishermen.

With the new information provided by Hakluyt adding to his own knowledge of Arctic navigation, Henry Hudson began to believe he knew the route of a northeast passage. Meanwhile, the Muscovy Company prepared to send a whaling fleet north to Spitsbergen to collect what they saw as endless renewable resources. Henry Hudson, who had delivered this opportunity to the company's directors, did not share in the fortune that the company soon accumulated: there would be no financial bonus for him.

Instead of offering him money, the directors of the Muscovy Company showed their appreciation for Hudson by inviting him to return to the Arctic again in 1608 on another voyage of exploration. Using the information and charts Hakluyt had provided him, Hudson led the directors to believe he had secret knowledge that would take him into the Kara Sea and safely through a northeast passage. Hudson, ever an opportunist, was once again showing his devious nature, this time to his employers.

Hopewell would again be Hudson's expedition ship. It was obvious he wasn't much of a bargainer, since his pay would be the same as for the previous voyage (said to have been a hundred pounds). This time, in accordance with his "secret" knowledge, Hudson was instructed to head past northern Norway for Novaya Zemlya, the gateway to the Kara Sea, and to seek a clear water route to Asia. Other explorers, British and Dutch (including Willem Barentsz), had reported on the ice-ridden waters that washed the western and northern coasts of Novaya Zemlya. Barentsz had even glimpsed the Kara Sea in the summer of 1594, but no one knew what might be found farther east. (Nearly three hundred years later, famed Norwegian Arctic explorer and sailor Fridtjof Nansen would refer to the waters beyond Novaya Zemlya as "the dreaded Kara Sea.")

Henry Hudson would not have lost heart no matter what the cost or how dreadful the Kara Sea might prove to be. He was determined to succeed where others had failed. He had already sailed farther north than Barentsz; now he would attempt to take a ship farther east into and through unknown waters.

The logo of the Muscovy Company (also called the Russian Company or Muscovy Trading Company), Hudson's employers for his first two Arctic voyages.

As on the previous polar voyage, John Hudson would sail with his father. Insisting he needed more crew, Hudson negotiated an agreement with the Muscovy Company for three additional crew members for the northeast-passage expedition. This brought the full complement to fifteen men. Among them were two men who would loom large in the future of Henry and John Hudson. One, Philip Staffe, was the carpenter. The other, signed on as first mate and somewhat older than Hudson and the rest of his crew, was

Robert Juet—a skilled seaman and navigator but other than that an unknown entity. The captain and mate clashed over Juet's sullen attitude and lack of consideration for the crew before the ship even left England: it was not an auspicious beginning for the second Arctic voyage.

After *Hopewell* had been reinforced with extra planking and sheathing, she left London on April 22, 1608. As usual, the North Sea weather proved less than kind. Fog and contrary winds slowed the ship down. Also, Hudson recorded that the carpenter got sick, and his illness was followed by four more crew going on the sick list. Captain Hudson and First Mate Robert Juet clashed again off the Norwegian coast. A stronger-minded captain would have taken Juet to task immediately, but Hudson neglected to do so; the scene was set for a dangerous situation if he could not get Juet under control.

In early June, later than expected, the ship was worked past Norway's North Cape. An intestinal bug of some kind must have been on board because the cook also got sick, along with another one of the crew. Meanwhile, the carpenter, recovered from his malady, fashioned a mast and sail for the ship's boat, which pleased the captain.

On the night of June 7, snow fell for four hours and was followed by a storm out of the northeast. The next day the weather cleared, although it remained very cold and stayed that way for a few more days. Ice came into view on June 12, spreading in an arc from northeast to northwest. The fair weather changed:

freezing fog enveloped the ship, and high winds whipped up the seas, keeping her lying ahull for hours. When the weather finally cleared again, a surprising event occurred.

On June 15, two of the seamen claimed to have seen a mermaid close up. Hudson actually reported this unlikely event in the official log, although he did not admit to having seen the creature himself. He wrote, "She was come close to the ships side, looking earnestly on the men: a little after, a sea came and overturned her: from the navel upward, her back and breasts were like a woman's, as they say that saw her; her body as big as one of us; her skin very white; and long hair hanging down behind, of colour black: in her going down they saw her tail, which was like the tail of a porpoise, and speckled like a mackerel." He added that the creature had been seen by Thomas Hills and Robert Raynor.

We know that mermaids do not exist. So what was it? Possibly it was an immature beluga whale or a large seal with seaweed caught around its neck. Over the next few days, the crew saw whales, porpoises, and many seabirds—but no more mermaids.

Ice loomed to the north and east; Hudson also recorded seeing ice to the northwest and the southeast. He entered the sighting in the log with additional observations: "I have some reason to think there is a tide or current setting to the northwards; the course we held and the way we made between this noon and midnight observations, does make me suspect it the more."

Hudson's crew heard polar bears roaring on the ice. ANTHONY DALTON

On June 20, polar bears were heard roaring on the ice, and the crew saw many seals. For the next week, progress was slow, constrained by pack ice and contrary winds. On June 27, they finally sighted Novaya Zemlya sprawled across their route. The Russian islands formed a bleak, frozen barrier stretching from the mainland far to the northeast.

The next day, under calm conditions, *Hopewell* took up a position two miles offshore Novaya Zemlya. Hudson sent Robert Juet and John Cooke ashore in the ship's boat with four other men to find fresh water and report what they could see on the land. They returned many hours later with an assortment of souvenirs, including deer horns and whale fins. They told Hudson of grass along the seashore and of boggy ground, typical of tundra. Although they did not encounter any wildlife, they did see the tracks of polar bears and deer and the much daintier prints of Arctic foxes. They reported seeing walruses in the sea; those on board had also seen walruses.

In order to help defray the costs of the expedition for his employers, Hudson hoped to kill walruses for their oil and their ivory tusks. That same day, Hudson allowed Juet to land again with seven men at a place where he felt the walruses would go ashore. They were disappointed but did not return empty-handed. On the shore, they found driftwood and a makeshift cross, which they took back to the ship with them. Other evidence of human presence was the discovery of some fireplaces. To help stock the ship's galley, the landing party gathered a dozen or more fowl and a clutch of eggs, many of which were found to be edible.

Many walruses approached the ship again on June 29. Knowing it was almost impossible to harvest any in the sea, Hudson tried once more to determine where they clambered ashore. Using oars and a sail, and towing one of the ship's boats behind *Hopewell,* they followed the walruses toward an inlet that appeared to be the mouth of a river flowing from the east. An abundance of ice flowed westward in the stream. *Hopewell* anchored off an island in the "river" mouth, from where the crew could see dozens of walruses stretched out on the ice.

By the next morning, as many as forty or fifty walruses

were sunning themselves on the rocky land and shore ice. With his mind on profit for the company, the captain sent most of the crew ashore in the shallop, with a musket each, to dispatch as many as possible and return with the ivory tusks. This proved to be an exercise in futility.

Having no apparent hunting skills and showing little in the way of common sense, the men raced up to the slumbering walruses, yelling and waving their arms, expecting little resistance. They were wrong in their assumptions—the canny beasts were too smart for the inexperienced Englishmen. As the sailors approached, the herd glided into the water and soon put themselves out of range. The disappointed "hunters" returned to face their captain's wrath with but one walrus head between them to show for their time and ammunition expenditure.

Seeing a bay with what looked like the entrance to a river on the southern shore of Novaya Zemlya on July 1, Hudson anchored *Hopewell* close to the opening, unaware that he had placed his ship in jeopardy: his anchorage was in a strong current that caught the ship in its grasp. Pulled by the current's powerful force, *Hopewell* dragged her anchor until she ran aground. The hull proved sound upon inspection, but even that news did not stop yet another flare-up between the captain and his first mate. In front of other crew members, Juet shouted at Hudson, accusing him of anchoring in an unsafe place and endangering the ship. Instead of admonishing Juet for his rudeness and insubordination,

The crew's attempt to hunt walruses was not a success; they came back to the ship with one head to show for their efforts. ANTHONY DALTON

Hudson took the easy way out: he ordered Juet to take some men and tow the ship off into deeper water. Juet did as he was told, but again damage had been done to the relationship between the two. Such a scene would not have helped the rest of the crew maintain confidence in their captain. Quarrels like this between the captain and one of his officers could only weaken Hudson's already fragile authority.

In his log, Hudson wrote that he had planned to force his way east through the wide strait known as Vaigats, between Novaya Zemlya and the Russian mainland, far to the south of the ship's current position. He maintained that getting through Vaigats was the key to reaching the mouth of the River Ob and then doubling the Cape of

Tartaria (also known at the time as Cape Taimur—almost certainly the location of today's Cape Severo-Vostochnoi) to get farther east. If it couldn't be done, there should be good reasons as to why it was not possible. In the summer of 1608, the problem with the Vaigats route was heavy ice crowded up against the mainland, preventing access to the strait. As an alternative, the more northerly route shown by the walrus herd intrigued Hudson enough to give it a try.

After attempting to sail *Hopewell* into the "river" but being beaten back by a combination of the strong current and a headwind, Hudson sent Juet and crew members in the shallop to explore farther east. They were gone for a day and a night. During their absence, Hudson tried again to force *Hopewell* east but made little headway. When Juet returned, he brought depressing information. About twenty-four miles to the east, the "river" depth shrunk to only a few feet. Juet told the captain the depth was not enough to float a ship the size of *Hopewell*. To Hudson, this was crushing news. Another voyage had come to a grinding halt. The Muscovy Company directors had spent a lot of money on the expedition, and this time, unlike his discovery of the Spitsbergen whale population on the North Pole expedition, Hudson had little to show them in return.

Neither Hudson nor Juet could have known it, but they were almost certainly in what is now known as Matochkin Strait, not a river. Although the narrow waterway is icebound for most of the year, it does, in fact, get deeper. It is possible that with a lot of effort, *Hopewell* could have been manoeuvred through the shallows and continued on to join the Kara Sea that Hudson sought—the sea that would have led him through the Northeast Passage to China.

Frustrated and disappointed yet again, Hudson spent a few more days cruising the coast, looking for an alternative way east. His ship was blocked by ice to the north and south, and by land—Novaya Zemlya—to the east. It was time to turn the ship around. First, though, he sent men ashore to hunt for food. They returned with nearly a hundred large birds, which he referred to as "wellocks" (probably a type of duck or goose).

After the crew had feasted on some of the fowl, Hudson ordered *Hopewell* turned to the west, telling his crew they were going home. After weeks in the icy-cold climate of the Russian Arctic, they were, no doubt, delighted at the news. The date was July 6, 1608.

That devious side of Hudson's nature then surfaced once more. Although the winds were variable and often contrary, *Hopewell* made good time from Novaya Zemlya to northern Norway and rounded North Cape on July 18 without incident. While heading south, abeam of the Lofoten Islands, Hudson made a subtle course change, turning the ship gradually to the west. Without telling the crew of his decision, he had decided to risk all by crossing the North Atlantic to search once again for a northwest passage.

When it became obvious about two weeks later that England was not their destination, *Hopewell*'s crew, almost certainly egged on by Robert Juet, threatened mutiny if Hudson did not turn the ship around. Thus, instead of returning to the Arctic and having to spend a miserable winter in a land of ice and snow, *Hopewell* and its crew arrived off Gravesend on August 26.

Before his men went ashore, Hudson gave each one a strange certificate of release from the ship. The wording for such an extraordinary event was recorded as the final paragraph for the voyage in the ship's log:

> The seventh of August, I used all diligence to arrive at London, and therefore now I gave my company [crew] a certificate under my hand, of my free and willing return, without persuasion or force of any one or more of them: for at my being at Novaya Zemlya, the sixth of July, void of hope for a North-east passage (except by the Vaigats for which I was not fitted to try or prove) I therefore resolved to use all means I could to sail to the North-west; considering the time and means we had, if the wind should friend us, as in the first part of our voyage it had done, and to make trial of that place called Lumley's Inlet [probably today's Frobisher Bay], and the furious overfall by Captain Davis, hoping to run into it one hundred leagues, and return as God should enable me. But now having spent more than half the time I had, and gone but the shortest part of the way, by means of contrary winds; I thought it my duty to save victuals, wages and tackle by my speedy return, and not by foolish rashness,

> the time being wasted, to lay more charge upon the action than necessity should compel, I arrived at Gravesend on the 26 of August.

That sounds like a man responding to pressure, hardly the response of a typical sea captain to his crew, unruly or otherwise.

The directors of the Muscovy Company read Henry Hudson's report with rapidly increasing anger. As far as they were concerned, the expedition had been an expensive failure. They wanted results, not excuses. Hudson tried to draw their anger away by offering to sail on their behalf in search of a northwest passage. The company, he was told, was not interested. And there the partnership ended. Hudson had failed in his second mission for the Muscovy Company, and he was out of work. He did, however, possess one thing of extreme importance—the most recent charts of a northeast passage as far as Novaya Zemlya. Could he now persuade other merchant enterprises to back him in a new expedition? It was worth a try: he had nothing to lose.

CHAPTER

4

A Contract with Dutch Merchants

HUDSON'S FAILURE TO FIND A navigable route through a northeast passage to China had greatly disappointed and displeased the directors of the Muscovy Company. After they dispensed with his services, he was then free to contact other potential masters. He knew he would have to work fast to procure a new commission to prevent another from beating him to the goal. Furthermore, as a sailor, Henry Hudson was not happy on the shore. He was a dedicated family man, but that aspect of his life would always be secondary to his life at sea.

Communications by letter were slow, but word of mouth was fast. Within a few days of being released by the Muscovy Company, the scuttlebutt around London and farther afield would have announced Captain Hudson's availability. Certainly, just across the North Sea, the Dutch heard about him, and Hudson knew in turn that they had offered a reward of twenty-five thousand guilders to the captain who could find a short sea route to China. It wasn't long before a Dutch diplomat approached Hudson on behalf of the Dutch East India Company (*De Vereenigde Oost-indische Compagnie*, or VOC). He was invited to Amsterdam, all expenses paid, to discuss an expedition across the top of the world.

Even though Hudson was in the Netherlands as their guest, the directors of the Dutch East India Company appeared to be in no hurry to meet the famous English explorer. They kept Hudson waiting in Amsterdam (at their expense) for over a week. Hudson spent his days wisely. He travelled to The Hague, where he visited the famed cartographer and theologian Peter Plancius, an associate of Richard Hakluyt.

Hudson and Plancius got along well. They knew a lot about each other, almost certainly through their mutual friend Hakluyt. Both were fascinated by maps of all kinds, particularly those that were incomplete. Sea charts would have been high on their list of topics for discussion, and the Arctic would have been foremost in their minds. After his failure to get through the ice and past Novaya Zemlya off the northern coast of Russia the previous year, Hudson was convinced there was no navigable route in that direction, and he said so to Plancius. The shortest route from Europe to China, he believed, was in the opposite direction, through the as yet undiscovered northwest passage.

When Hudson was finally called before three of the VOC's directors—Dirk van Os, Isaac Le Maire, and Jan Poppe—he exhibited a complete about-face, perhaps warned to do so by Plancius. Ignoring his recent private revelations to the Dutch cartographer, Hudson tucked all thoughts of a northwest passage away in his mind. Instead, he considered where the money expected him to look.

"Could he, Henry Hudson, find a route through the northeast passage?" was the essence of the most important question asked that day. Hudson replied yes and then expanded on his apparent beliefs for an hour or more, using his charts and describing the ice and its movements. Having spent a few weeks sailing the Arctic coast of Russia the previous year, he was able to make a convincing presentation. Although he had not seen it, he knew that the Vaigats Strait at the southern end of Novaya Zemlya should lead to the Kara Sea. The problem for a sailing ship was that the approaches to the strait, and the strait itself, were always choked with ice. Hudson admitted to the VOC that he didn't know the exact whereabouts of a navigable opening to the elusive northeast passage, but he did know where not to look. The presentation may have been short on answers, but it was padded with enough detail to be impressive.

The shipbuilding yard of the Dutch East India Company (*De Vereenigde Oost-indische Compagnie*, or VOC) in Amsterdam.
STADSARCHIEF AMSTERDAM/JOSEPH MULDER

Having stated his case and collected money for his expenses, Hudson was free to go home and wait for a decision. He had no idea how long that would take or even if he would be chosen for the role of captain. All he could do at that time was to hope for the best. Before he left for England, Hudson again visited Peter Plancius at his home in The Hague.

About that time, or soon after, the French began to make overtures to Hudson for a similar Arctic expedition, but those talks—if indeed the two parties got as far as talking—

came to nothing. However, a long letter on the subject does exist. It was written by Pierre Jeannin, the president of the Parliament of Burgundy, to King Henry IV of France and dated January 21, 1609. The letter was intended to remind the king of the urgency of the matter, as expressed to Jeannin by Le Maire.

Jeannin, under the king's orders, he said, had for some time been working on the financial logistics of a possible Arctic expedition with VOC director Isaac Le Maire. The plan was to employ a noted explorer, such as Henry Hudson. Isaac Le Maire, who had met Hudson, did not have any discussions with the latter. To distance himself from the project, due to his involvement with the VOC, he enlisted the help of his own brother, Jacob, to be the intermediary. The problem was that King Henry took too long to make a decision.

Sometime in January 1609, Hudson was again called to Amsterdam by the VOC. There he learned his proposal had been accepted. He was invited to sign a contract to captain a voyage in search of a northeast passage. Nowhere among the many clauses was there any indication that Hudson could wander off in any other direction if the mood so took him. Whether he liked it or not, his focus was to be to the east.

Given the task of returning to Novaya Zemlya and again searching for a passage past the islands' icy barrier to reach the Kara Sea, Hudson prepared to set sail again, this time with two Dutch ships: *Half Moon* (*Halve Maen* in Dutch) and *Good Hope.* For defence against unfriendly Natives, or

The logo of *De Vereenigde Oost-indische Compagnie*, or VOC

pirates, *Half Moon* was armed with six cannons—two on either side, with another pair of smaller guns over the stern. No details are available for *Good Hope.* In fact, *Good Hope* is never mentioned again, certainly not in Hudson's log of the voyage nor in that of his mate, Robert Juet. Where and when, whether early or late in the voyage, the two ships parted company is unknown. *Good Hope* simply vanished from the history of Hudson's third Arctic voyage.

As soon as he saw her, Hudson knew the small three-masted, square-rigged *Half Moon*, built with a flat bottom, would have a hard time in the Arctic ice, but he had no alternative. The company directors told him, in effect, to "take it or leave it." Hudson could not turn down the opportunity.

The choice of officers and crew would be up to Captain Hudson, as was customary at the time. Hiring crews was a simple task: unemployed sailors were easy to find at almost any seaport in the world. Hudson had no trouble finding such men along the Thames River in London. Finding suitable officers was a different matter.

Inexplicably, Hudson invited Robert Juet to sail with him again—possibly as the first mate, but certainly as an extra navigator, because Juet was a competent astronomer skilled in celestial navigation. It was a union doomed to failure, as it had been in 1608. Perhaps Hudson felt that Juet had some sort of hold over him—possibly the reason for issuing the certificates to the crew of *Hopewell* at the end of that voyage the previous year. Although that may or may not have swayed Hudson's decision, it is more difficult to speculate about Juet's decision to accept Hudson's offer. Unless it was for the money, why would he go to sea again with a captain he disliked and for whom he had no respect? He had not enjoyed sailing with Captain Hudson on *Hopewell*, and he was unlikely to be any happier as mate aboard *Half Moon*.

John Colman, who had served Hudson well as first mate on the 1607 voyage, signed on again, possibly as bosun, for the *Half Moon* expedition. He was no doubt lured by the relatively high wages Hudson was offering.

The duplicitous side of Hudson's character once again took over. At this time, well before his departure for the Arctic, Hudson had already planned to deceive his new employers. Instead of sailing north and east after leaving Amsterdam, he intended to set course in the opposite direction and cross the North Atlantic in the hope of finding a northwest passage. He must have confided this objective to either Robert Juet or John Colman—perhaps both—because someone let out the secret. Through waterfront gossip, the Dutch learned of the captain's real plans. The furious VOC directors confronted him with their discovery. To keep the job he wanted so badly, Hudson was forced to swear on the Bible that he would sail north and east as directed.

Beyond the two officers mentioned, *Half Moon*'s crew contained a volatile mix of English and Dutch sailors, the latter insisted on by the VOC. With their countries often at war with each other, the two groups did not get on at all well in the close confines of the sailing vessel. The crew consisted of Hudson's son John, a few English sailors, and a similar number of Dutch sailors—the actual numbers are unknown. By the time the officers and crew were assembled, it is believed they numbered sixteen in all. The Dutch and English sailors were so different from each other that any possibility of below-decks harmony was washed overboard with the first North Sea wave. They didn't speak the same language; they didn't eat the same food; they did not like each other. The cramped ship, only eighty-five feet long and about seventeen feet beam, became a festering breeding ground for dissension and possibly mutiny.

CHAPTER

5

The Long Voyage of *Half Moon*

APRIL 6, 1609. THE LAST of the crew straggled aboard and stowed their meagre belongings in the fo'c'sle. With the tide in his favour, Captain Hudson gave the order to cast off. Slowly at first, then with a little more speed, *Half Moon* sailed away from Amsterdam. The departure was badly timed for some of the sailors who had been ashore too long. As she entered the North Sea off the Dutch coast, *Half Moon* was hit by a major storm blasting in from the northwest. The storm built the waves into liquid mountains and soon had *Half Moon* rolling in stomach-churning arcs.

The crew, seasick or not, now had a chance to see what kind of a man their captain would prove to be. Hudson earned the respect of both English and Dutch sailors by staying on

A replica of *Half Moon* being towed on the Amstel River prior to being shipped to the US. NATIONAAL ARCHIEF/COLLECTIE SPAARNESTAD PHOTO/ FOTOGRAAF ONBEKEND, VIA NATIONAAL ARCHIEF

deck throughout the storm and handling the ship with an easy confidence that spoke much for his experience. The knowledge that Captain Hudson was a capable mariner helped, but it did nothing to improve relations between the two nationalities on board. Fights were commonplace. Adding to that problem (and despite his commanding presence during the storm), Hudson soon showed he was not good at maintaining the respect of his crew.

The Dutch sailors, used to the warm climate of voyages through the tropics to the East Indies, did not appreciate the cold Arctic air as the ship fought her way north. They only worked on deck and in the freezing rigging when they were forced to, which was rarely, because Hudson failed to command them properly. Since the Dutch found ways to avoid working in the cold, the English sailors had to take on the brunt of the daily tasks on deck and in the rigging, adding yet more fuel to the animosity on board. Contributing to the unrest, the cook is believed to have been Dutch and would therefore have cooked the meals according to Dutch tastes, with the emphasis on salted herring—not the kind of food enjoyed by English sailors, who preferred to eat beef, either salted or pickled.

It is unfortunate that Henry Hudson's log of the voyage has long since disappeared. Instead of the master's account, we have to rely on Robert Juet's personal journal—a clinical account of the voyage without personal comments and without mention of the crew and their daily routine. Juet's account also has obvious gaps. For example, he failed to record anything of the long haul up the North Sea toward Norway's North Cape. He passed that section of the voyage off with a casual "and because it is a journey usually known, I omit to put down what passed."

Juet takes up the tale off the North Cape, on May 6, but only to comment that "at twelve of the clock [noon], the North Cape did bear Southwest and by South, ten leagues off, and we steered away East and by South, and East."

Then there are two weeks unaccounted for—from May 6 to May 19, 1609. During those thirteen days, *Half Moon* sailed beyond the North Cape and worked east along

Russia's north coast. All Juet wrote of this time was the sighting of a sunspot—the first known sighting of this phenomenon—and a note that read, "After much trouble with fog, sometimes, and more dangers from ice . . . " He wrote this entry at the end of the missing thirteen days.

Assuming the ship reached the vicinity of Novaya Zemlya, she would have been stopped by ice, as *Hopewell* had been on Hudson's previous voyage to find the Kara Sea. The floes and shore-bound ice would have stretched as far as the eye could see along the length of Novaya Zemlya. We know that Hudson did not want to explore the seas beyond Novaya Zemlya; he had told Plancius he did not believe there was a navigable route beyond to China. His heart was set on finding a northwest passage. So, once they reached the blockade of ice at Novaya Zemlya, did he talk to his officers and crew and convince them to turn about and sail west across the Atlantic?

Another possibility is that the crew mutinied when they found the ship blocked by ice. If this was what happened, they were probably led by Robert Juet. The likelihood of mutiny is strong and was first mentioned by the Flemish historian Emanuel van Meteren (1535–1612). He wrote in *Historie der Nederlanden* that Hudson visited him after the 1609 voyage, showing van Meteren his logs, journals, and charts and telling him there had been a mutiny near Novaya Zemlya. Once confronted by thick ice, the crew, Hudson claimed, had refused to continue and demanded the ship be turned around.

At this point we have to rely on supposition. If the crew refused to attempt to sail farther east into the ice, even if open water could be found, the captain could have quelled the mutiny using his authority and backed by force of arms. But that was not Hudson's style. If there was a threat of mutiny, that would have served his purpose all too well. We do know from Juet's journal that once the ship reached the icy north coast of Russia, Hudson looked again to the distant west and ordered the helmsman to steer a new course. There is no mention in Juet's report of Hudson's reasons for aborting the mission to find a northeast passage and no mention of a mutiny. We don't know how close the ship was to Novaya Zemlya, but based on the dates in Juet's log, she was closer to North Cape when Hudson turned her around.

Juet wrote of the weather as the ship turned in her own wake and sailed back toward North Cape, "The nineteenth [of May], being Tuesday, was close stormy weather, with much wind and snow and very cold: the wind variable between the North Northwest and Northeast." He also wrote of the ship being held up by contrary winds east of North Cape and unable to get past the headland until May 21. There is something incongruous about these dates, since *Half Moon* could not have sailed from the vicinity of Novaya Zemlya to North Cape in such a limited time. It could be, however, that the two weeks of May missing from Juet's log accounted for *Half Moon*'s voyage toward Novaya Zemlya and back to the cape—and a possible mutiny.

Historians have speculated that at this point in the voyage, Hudson might have offered his crew of malcontents a couple of choices. They could sail for Holland and be hanged as mutineers in Amsterdam—as they most certainly would have been—or they could set course across the Atlantic and search for a northwest passage. Once close to the western side, they would again have two options. They could either sail up the western coast of Greenland, cross Davis Strait, and attempt the west-reaching strait known as the Furious Overfall (later to be named Hudson Strait), or they could follow a more southerly course. Captain John Smith (of Pocahontas fame), a younger associate of Hudson's, had spoken of his belief that a northwest passage might be reached from a point near latitude 40° north, where a river flowed from out of the northwest.

So, hanging or freedom? If that was what Hudson offered his crew, it wasn't much of a choice. The men would most likely have chosen to follow their captain toward the New World. As the ship turned west, *Half Moon*'s crew believed they were sailing away from the ice for warmer seas, and they settled down. But the going wasn't that simple. First, *Half Moon* could not get past North Cape. Winds played with her, holding her back. Then the weather improved until the ship neared the Lofoten Islands; there, a storm hit. The northern route across the North Atlantic can be rough at the best of times, and May 1609 was no exception. Even so, for the crew, it was better than battling Arctic ice.

Caught by the storm far north of Scotland's Shetland Islands on May 25, *Half Moon* rolled and lurched over the whitecaps toward the Faroes. Pelting the ship with snow and icy hail, the squall lasted for the best part of three days, reaching its peak on May 26. Juet noted that with minimum sails (probably just a mizzen for stability), the storm still carried the ship "seventy leagues in four and twenty hours." That's just over 182 nautical miles, driven by the wind.

When the weather had calmed down, Hudson had the crew set the mainsail, spritsail, and main topsail. Two days later, with smooth seas and little wind, they sighted the Faroes. A note in the log recorded that the island group was nearly forty nautical miles west of the position on the chart—a rather strange observation, considering that Hudson had called at the Faroes on the way home from Spitsbergen in 1607 and had not then mentioned the discrepancy between his charts and the true location.

On May 29, with the tide ebbing and the wind against her, *Half Moon* was unable to approach the land, so she stood off from the shore and waited until the following morning. By nine o'clock, the crew had found a decent anchorage, and a boat was sent ashore. Juet wrote that Captain Hudson went along that morning for a walk with some of the crew.

After taking on water, fresh vegetables, and half a dozen live sheep from the misty islands, *Half Moon* resumed the voyage. Hudson's first objective was to locate Buss Island, reportedly seen from one of Sir Martin Frobisher's ships in 1578. *Half Moon*'s captain and crew were unsuccessful, because Buss Island does not exist: it was a figment of someone's imagination or, perhaps, a trick of the light.

At first the Atlantic weather played fair with the ship and crew. It could not last. Within a few days of leaving the Faroes, *Half Moon* ran into "much wind with fog and rain." The wind increased throughout the day, so Hudson ordered the topsail taken in. At four the following morning, they reduced sail again and hove to under mainsail alone, the better to ride out the storm. Over the next few days, the winds varied in strength and direction. By the afternoon of June 7, a full gale blew out of the northwest.

The weather continued to ply the ship with alternating winds—sometimes gentle, sometimes gale force. *Half Moon* was experiencing typical North Atlantic weather patterns—clear skies, gentle winds, and calm seas interspersed with thick fog and sudden gales lasting anywhere from a few hours to a day or two. One violent storm, which blasted the ship for four terrifying days, sent the foremast overboard as it attacked the sailors with icy intensity. On June 21, the wind blew hard enough to split the foresail in mid-morning. While the crew repaired the damage, *Half Moon* continued under mainsail alone.

Once the ship reached the west side of the Atlantic, Hudson decided to explore south along the North American coast and search for the river John Smith had mentioned to him in England. In doing so, he spared his men the trials of another cold and frightening sojourn in the Arctic.

On the Grand Banks off southeast Newfoundland, the variable winds carried *Half Moon* on an erratic series of courses from July 2 through July 10. On July 8, Hudson took advantage of better weather to load the ship with as many cod as his men could catch. The tally? One hundred and eighteen fish in one morning, according to Juet, and another twelve or so later in the day, gave the sailors something else to think about as they gutted and salted them—some to eat on board, most for eventual sale. They also saw many large schools of herring.

To their surprise, they were not alone. A fleet of French fishing boats was also working the Grand Banks, but there was no contact between them and *Half Moon*. The men did speak with the crew of a lone French vessel a few days later, near Sable Island.

With her new cargo safe in the hold, *Half Moon* followed a course that took her close to the land, southwest of present-day Lunenburg, Nova Scotia, on July 12. Juet described the coast as "low white sandie ground." From there, the little sailing ship crossed the Gulf of Maine to make landfall near Penobscot Bay. En route, Juet caught another fifteen cod, which he described as "some of the greatest I have ever seen." Close to the land, two boats manned by six Natives (or "savages," as Juet referred to them) came out to the ship to trade.

Up to this time Hudson had only left his ship once since

sailing from Amsterdam many weeks earlier, and that for only an hour or so in the Faroes. On July 18, 1609, he went ashore on North American soil for the first time. Having lost his foremast in the storm southwest of the Faroes, he had his men cut a tall, straight tree from the abundant forests and trim it to size.

It is surprising that Juet rarely mentions Captain Hudson in his journal, which is mainly a clear and simple account of weather conditions, directions sailed, latitudes crossed, and landmarks noted, with few personal references of any kind. A reader gets the sense at times that Juet believed himself to be in sole charge of the ship and crew: while out at sea, he often describes what he has done and what he has observed but rarely refers to anyone else.

For the next few days, while the new mast was being prepared by the carpenter on the shore, Juet and the crew kept busy. With the ship at anchor, some men went out fishing in a small boat. They returned with an excellent haul of 31 lobsters. A day later, they brought in 27 large cod and another 40 lobsters; the crew was in a seafood heaven. Another day saw 59 more lobsters brought on board. The men also caught many more large cod and a big halibut.

While *Half Moon* was anchored, two French ships sailed in carrying many Native people but did not offer Hudson or his men any cause for alarm. Despite that, the crew on *Half Moon* were uneasy and concerned for their own safety. That concern was soon translated into action when twelve men armed with muskets, Juet among them, went ashore and raided the Native village. The Europeans dragged the Native people from their homes and, in Juet's words, "took spoyle of them, as they would have done of us."

The attack on the village was unprovoked and quite pointless. It is a sobering example of the brutality European sailors and explorers of the era habitually showed the indigenous peoples they encountered in far-off lands. On this voyage, it would not be the last time Juet was guilty of assault or murder, warranted or otherwise. Immediately after the raiders returned to the ship, *Half Moon* hauled anchor and set sail. She didn't get far: mist, rain, and a headwind held them at the harbour mouth until midnight. Then the wind relented and the mist cleared. Soon *Half Moon* was under sail again and proceeding south-southwest.

Half Moon sighted the promontory we now call Cape Cod on August 3, and a few men went ashore, where they found grapes and wild roses. Difficult currents and riptides over an inconsistent seabed, and gale-force winds, kept the ship moving on a triangular course that night. By daybreak the cape was still close by, and voices could be heard on the land. Hudson sent a boat ashore to investigate; it returned with a Native on board. He was given a few trinkets and a meal before being taken back to shore.

Juet commented in his log, "The land is very sweet," adding, "The people have green tobacco and pipes, the boles whereof are made of Earth, and the pipes of red copper."

The shallop was badly damaged on August 9 when it crashed into *Half Moon*'s stern while it was being towed. The collision wrecked the smaller boat's stem. Hudson ordered the wreckage to be cut away and abandoned. *Half Moon* probably carried one or two rowing boats and a shallop, so would still have had a small boat available to take men ashore when required.

Half Moon continued along the coast, always toward the south, with the crew taking regular soundings and making directional observations throughout the days and nights. The weather varied from warm breezes and calm seas to sudden gales. By August 18 the ship was crossing the bar that protected Chesapeake Bay and what Juet referred to as the King's River (James River) in Virginia, where there was a colony of English settlers.

Tacking back and forth and continuing to take soundings, Hudson kept *Half Moon* moving south until she was abeam of today's Cape Hatteras on August 24. On that date, he turned his ship north again, following the coast to Delaware Bay, which he reached three days later. *Half Moon* sailed into the bay, where Juet recorded seeing the mouths of many rivers, but shoal water caused the ship to return to the ocean. Shoals now kept the ship offshore for a few days until they stood in toward a magnificent natural harbour on September 2. Hudson thought it might be a huge lake or a vast bay bordered by flat land and a few low-lying hills. At the head of the bay, a long, narrow island stood in the mouth of a river. The following morning, Hudson found he had a choice of "three great rivers." The most northerly proved to have a shoal and a bar across it. He moved to the south and anchored. That day the men went fishing and caught ten large mullets and a giant ray that was so heavy, Juet wrote, it took four men to haul it on board.

The outflow of water, a combination of river currents and tidal flow, suggested to Hudson that he might be close to the river Captain John Smith had described, the one thought to lead to China and the riches of Asia. It would have been an exciting moment for him.

Native people came out to the ship out of curiosity and with hopes of trading. They were friendly and carried with them tobacco, which they willingly bartered for beads, knives, and clothes, but they went home before nightfall. They returned the next day in greater numbers and with more tobacco. Although they showed no aggression on either occasion, Hudson's men were nervous. They kept a diligent watch that night.

Hudson sent out John Colman and four other men in a small boat on September 6 with instructions to explore a narrow river nearby that cut through high ground. On the way back to the ship, Colman's party was attacked by four Native people in two canoes. Colman was killed in the fight by an arrow through his throat. His companions, two of whom were hurt in the short battle, had to spend the night in the boat, on open water, because they could not find the ship in the dark. They finally returned to *Half Moon* in mid-morning. John Colman was buried on the shore.

Although friendly Natives came out to the ship again, the crew found it impossible to trust them. Their fears were confirmed when two large canoes, both filled with heavily armed men, approached. Hudson allowed most of the friendly traders to leave the ship but kept one man as security. It was a wasted effort: he jumped overboard soon after and escaped ashore.

On September 11, Hudson moved his ship into the river that Colman had looked at. It seemed to be navigable for a ship of *Half Moon*'s size and a good bet for exploring the interior. The Natives knew the river as Cahohatatea, which would one day become known as the Hudson River. The long island to starboard, which they had seen on September 2 and which the Native people called Mannahata, would eventually become Manhattan Island.

Half Moon now ventured into the interior of the continent. For the next few days after Colman's death, Hudson and crew were cautious in dealing with the locals, most of whom wanted only to trade. *Half Moon* continued along the beautiful river valley, the crew enjoying the impressive views of the 20-mile (32-kilometre) stretch of cliffs on the west side, now known as the Palisades. Rising almost sheer from the river, the cliffs vary from 300 feet (91 metres) in height to more than 500 feet (152 metres). In his log, Juet referred to the cliffs as mountains.

Natives watch from shore as *Half Moon* passes on the Hudson River. LIBRARY OF CONGRESS 3A06608U

September 12 was hot and humid, with calm conditions over the river. Two dozen canoes appeared, carrying more Native people to the ship to trade, but Hudson would not allow any of them on board. He did allow the cook to buy oysters and beans from the visitors, who were obviously armed. As they progressed upriver, the crew of *Half Moon* fished and explored the land along the banks and took depth soundings out in the stream most days. Day after day, canoes came out with Native men, women, and children aboard. Each time, Hudson and his men allowed them to trade but not to come on board until, on September 21, he invited some of the chiefs on deck, along with one of their wives. He and Juet plied them with wine in the captain's cabin in an attempt to discover whether they were friends or foes. Not surprisingly, the Natives—unaccustomed to alcohol—were soon intoxicated. But they did go ashore again at nightfall, happy and in peace.

Despite the successful visit by the local chiefs, none of Hudson's men could afford to trust the Native people entirely. A few of the locals were allowed on board most days but were always watched with suspicion.

On September 22, Hudson sent a boat upriver from their anchorage to take soundings; the men returned with depressing news. Within a few miles, the river shallowed, making it impossible for *Half Moon* to go any farther. The river flowed from the north, stretching over three hundred miles from its source to the Atlantic. Its direction was not exactly the one Hudson wanted, but it was close. Now, after the ship had travelled some hundred and fifty miles upstream, the river had effectively become a dead end. Hudson and *Half Moon* had to turn around, having reached the approximate location of present-day Albany. Had he gone a few miles farther, Hudson would have found the confluence with the Mohawk River, which flowed from the northwest but still would not have been navigable for a ship the size of *Half Moon*. (Although he would be unaware of it, of course, the Hudson River and roadways on both sides of it would eventually be named for him.)

Hudson was disappointed at not being able to go any farther, but he wasn't ready to give up his quest. Deep inside, he knew there was a way to China past the Americas—if only he could find it.

The Italian explorer Giovanni da Verrazzano had seen the mouth of this river in 1524 but had not sailed up it to determine its length or direction. Verrazzano is, however, credited with the discovery of New York Harbor. Like Hudson, he has been memorialized for his discoveries: Verrazzano's name is on the narrow entrance to New York Harbor and the bridge that spans it.

On the way downriver to the open ocean, the ship ran aground a couple of times on mud flats and had to wait for high water before it could be floated off. Hudson and his crew had many more encounters with Native people, some pleasant, a few blatant attacks. One Native managed to climb into the ship through a window in the stern and steal a few items. Juet shot and killed him as he tried to make his escape. Other Natives near the ship fled, some by canoe, others by swimming. Meanwhile, some of the crew took to a small boat, intending to recover the stolen items. One Native, perhaps bolder than the rest, grabbed hold of the boat and tried to turn it over. The ship's cook cut off the Native's hand with his sword and pushed him into the river, where he drowned.

Half Moon stood at anchor that night in the middle of the river. It proved to be a quiet night, but all that changed with the coming of daylight. Two canoes filled with hostile Natives armed with bows and arrows approached the ship. Hudson's crew loaded their muskets and shot at them, killing two or three. The others paddled back to shore. They were soon joined by up to a hundred more Natives, who fired on the ship from the shore. *Half Moon*'s smallest cannon was called into use and returned the fire, killing at least one. The others fled into the forest. Another canoe came out loaded with warriors, and again the small cannon fired. More Natives fell. The sailing ship's crew fired muskets and killed a few more of their assailants before the anchor was hauled up and the ship got under way. The fight was over. *Half Moon* continued her journey downstream to the large natural harbour from which they had started the river journey without additional trouble from Native people.

On October 4, as the sun reached its zenith, Hudson called for all sails to be set. *Half Moon* dipped her bowsprit toward the open ocean and made ready for the long crossing to Europe. By this time the Dutch East India Company directors would be expecting news of him and his discoveries. For Hudson, it was getting close to the time he would have to confront his employers.

Half Moon on the Hudson River, adapted from a painting by Will Crawford. LIBRARY OF CONGRESS 26414R

Robert Juet completed his log of the long voyage with a single short paragraph: "We continued our course toward England, without seeing any land by the way, all the rest of this month of October: and on the seventh day of November . . . being Saturday, by the Grace of God we arrived safely in the range of Dartmouth in Devonshire, in the year 1609."

That last entry is a clear and concise ending to the story of Hudson's third voyage, but it is, again, only part of the truth. It appears Juet deliberately neglected to record all that happened.

Somewhere between leaving American shores and

arriving in England, *Half Moon*'s crew again threatened mutiny, an event Emanuel van Meteren recorded in his *Historie der Nederlanden.* Hudson had taken *Half Moon* into Dartmouth so that the crew could avoid the Dutch authorities. He had planned to spend the winter there and continue his search for a northwest passage in the spring of 1610.

While in Dartmouth, he wrote to his masters in Amsterdam, telling them of his finds across the ocean. They ordered him to return to Amsterdam immediately with their ship and explain himself. Hudson could not do that, since King James I had forbidden him (and the English members of his crew) to leave the country pending an inquiry into possible treason for working with the Dutch against English interests. Hudson therefore ignored the Dutch order and travelled to London to spend Christmas with his family. His crew members are not mentioned in van Meteren's book, but it is probable that some of them stayed with the ship for a few months until it was finally allowed to sail to Amsterdam in July 1610. Captain Hudson did not return to Amsterdam with his ship. By then he was already back at sea, sailing in the opposite direction, on an English ship.

CHAPTER

6

In Search of a Northwest Passage, Again

BECAUSE HENRY HUDSON WAS AN Englishman who had been employed by the Dutch, his own countrymen suspected him of disloyalty, even treason. He soon found himself in the unenviable position of being a diplomatic pawn, pulled on one side by Dutch interests and on the other by British needs. If he could stay out of prison, the eventual result appeared to be a win-win situation for him. In this case, he was lucky. His fame (or perhaps his notoriety) earned him the captaincy of the English ship *Discovery*. His instructions from the three British businessmen who employed him were simple: search for and find a northwest passage through to China. Hudson's benefactors were Sir Dudley Digges, Sir Thomas Smythe, and Sir John Wolstenholme.

The first attempt to find a navigable northern sea route to China had been made by an Italian, John Cabot, in 1497. Despite his nationality, Cabot had been working for English interests. He sailed as far as Newfoundland and returned to England safely. The following year he set course for the west again. This time, with instructions from King Henry VII, he was to search even farther. Cabot left Bristol with five ships. Weeks later, one storm-ravaged vessel staggered into an Irish port. The other four, with Captain John Cabot and his crews, were never heard from again.

John Cabot's son Sebastian, an experienced navigator like his father, went looking for a northwest passage in 1509, with two ships. Although he is said to have taken a look at Hudson Strait, which he called Rio Nevado, he went no farther and returned to Europe with only wild stories to relate. He made another attempt to earn sponsorship for a new expedition in 1521 but was unable to build enough financial interest.

King Henry VIII financed two ships in 1527, with instructions to the expedition's master, a Captain Rut, to find a route over the North Pole to China. One ship went down after being pounded by an Atlantic storm. The other reached the North American continent somewhere in the region of Nova Scotia and sailed south to the Caribbean before returning to England the following year. Rut had accomplished nothing new.

Many others searched for a short sea route to China;

none were successful. Jacques Cartier discovered what is now the St. Lawrence River in 1535, on his second expedition to the New World. He reached Hochelaga, site of present-day Montreal, before being stopped by the impassable Lachine Rapids.

Sir Humphrey Gilbert (a half-brother of Sir Walter Raleigh) was a staunch advocate of an expedition to search for a northwest passage. His eloquent arguments convinced investors to send out Martin Frobisher, a former pirate, in 1576. Frobisher actually came close to solving the puzzle of where the passage started but failed because he allowed himself to be distracted by the thought of gold. Frobisher sailed deep into a sound, or bay, that he named after himself. He thought it was a strait and the possible gateway to China, so he named it Frobisher's Straite. Today we know it as Frobisher Bay.

Frobisher made a second voyage to his strait in 1577 and a third in 1578. During the latter expedition, unable to get into his eponymous strait due to ice concentration, he and his ship sailed deep into what is now Hudson Strait. He is said to have spent almost three weeks pushing his ship westward until forced back by fog and a strong current setting to the east. That current flows from Fury and Hecla Strait into and through Foxe Basin and so to Hudson Strait. Frobisher was on the right track, but even had he continued, he would never have been successful. Fury and Hecla Strait is choked by heavy ice almost year round, and no sixteenth-century wooden sailing ship could possibly have navigated through its frozen turbulence to the Gulf of Boothia. Even so, despite its dangers and its other drawbacks, if the ice ever clears it is one of the sea routes that could be a northwest passage.

In 1602, another Englishman, Sir George Weymouth, commanded a two-ship expedition (one ship was *Discovery*) to probe farther into "Frobisher's Straite." Although he took his ships deep into the long inlet, he did not go far enough to establish that he was, in fact, proceeding to a dead end. Weymouth did cross the turbulent mouth of Hudson Strait on his return voyage.

Thanks to his friendship with Richard Hakluyt, Hudson was able to study George Weymouth's updated charts of the waters between Greenland and the Furious Overfall.

Hudson sailed for the Subarctic from England April 17, 1610, on *Discovery*. The ship departed St. Katherine's Dock in the heart of London and sailed downstream the few miles as far as Blackwall to wait until the weather improved. From there she continued on the meandering Thames toward the open sea. On board were twenty-one men and two boys, one of whom was Henry Hudson's son John, who was on his third voyage with his father. The other youngster was cabin boy Nicholas Simms. Robert Juet was again on board—but as second, not first, mate. That position had gone to a William Coleburne, on the orders of the sponsors. There is a sense that Hudson was not happy with this arrangement. Off the Isle of Sheppey, he sent William Coleburne back to London on a passing ship. In his journal, Hudson said that Coleburne carried a letter from him to the expedition's financial backers explaining the reason for Coleburne's dismissal. If that is so, the letter and its contents have long since been lost. Why a ship's officer such as Coleburne was dismissed from the ship so early in the voyage is unknown. Presumably, it was simply an excuse for Hudson to rid the ship of a potential company spy—or an otherwise unwanted nuisance. Coleburne's abrupt departure moved Robert Juet back up into his customary position as first mate. With that promotion, Hudson again endangered his own authority.

As with Hudson's third voyage, little material is available written by Hudson himself concerning the fourth voyage. A brief extract exists, but it covers only the barest details between the departure from England and the ship's arrival at the entrance to Hudson Bay after working through Hudson Strait. For a detailed record of the voyage, we have to rely on the journal of Abacuck Prickett. This work is, of necessity, a biased account. Prickett had been placed on board as a crew member by his employer, Sir Dudley Digges, to report on the voyage. Compared to the rest of the crew, Prickett was a reasonably educated man—which meant he could read and write. In light of the events that would take place in James Bay in 1611, he had every reason to sanitize his journal.

Off the Isle of Sheppey, still within the Thames River estuary, two more men came aboard *Discovery*. One was a visitor who left the ship a few days later at Harwich, on

England's east coast. The other was a young friend of Henry Hudson's named Henry Greene. He remained on board when the ship sailed out of Harwich for the Arctic.

Hudson's summary of the voyage mentions getting rid of Coleburne but does not allude to Greene joining the ship, nor the stop at Harwich.

Discovery sailed north from Harwich, passing the great chalk cliffs of Flamborough Head, Yorkshire, on May 2. Three days later she came abreast of the Orkney Islands. After passing the islands, she turned northwest, making her way across the North Atlantic, first toward the Faroe Islands. Although Hudson had visited the Faroes on his ocean crossing in *Half Moon*, on this voyage he passed them with no more than a note in the log recording the date and latitude.

Discovery continued to the southeast coast of Iceland, where she dropped anchor. After more than three weeks at sea in the small ship, the crew would have welcomed the opportunity to go ashore and hunt birds for a few days. They also spent some of their time at anchor fishing for cod, ling, and halibut. Hudson wrote to a friend about the abundance of game birds on the land, of which, he said, he shot over twenty.

The lengthy stopover was for more than a rest and to reprovision the ship; there was ice up against the coast to the west.

As May turned into June and the ice began to break

up, *Discovery* hauled anchor and continued to the west. Abacuck Prickett recorded seeing Iceland's Mount Hecla spewing hot lava into the air as they passed. Inclement weather and fields of drifting ice sent *Discovery* to anchor again, this time near Iceland's northwest corner. On land, the crew enjoyed cleansing themselves and, for many of them, washing their lice-ridden clothes in a natural pool of hot water. Prickett noted that the water was "so hot it would scald a fowl." The crew employed their collective sense of humour to name the location Lousy Bay.

The brief stopover in Iceland was not completely peaceful. Henry Greene picked a fight with Edward Wilson, the ship's young surgeon, over possession of a game bird one of them had shot. Greene beat Wilson severely. The result was that the surgeon refused to leave Iceland with the ship and had to be persuaded by most of the crew to continue with them. Although Prickett informed Hudson of the incident, the captain chose not to do anything about the fight, even though Wilson was an officer and Greene was his subordinate.

Four days beyond Iceland, many of the crew saw the towering snow-covered rocks and glaciers of Greenland for the first time. By then they were navigating through fields of broken ice and dodging icebergs. Robert Juet, a man who should have been a responsible second-in-command, now began to stir the crew up against the captain; it was by then a familiar pattern for Juet. Apparently referring to the fight in Iceland between Greene and Wilson and the captain's avoidance of the issue, he is reported to have said to at least two crew members, "There'll be bloodshed aboard this ship before the voyage is over . . . " It proved to be a realistic forecast.

Once the ship had passed the southern tip of Greenland and was heading north, three whales approached. Two passed very close and one swam under the ship, though without damaging it.

For the next few days, in the southern limits of Davis Strait, Hudson steered an erratic course, sometimes northwest, sometimes southwest, to keep clear of the ice drifting in and out of the fog. On June 25, lookouts saw land to the west. They had reached Resolution Island, the northern gateway to the Furious Overfall and beyond to what is now Hudson Bay.

The long stretch of turbulent ice and water that Captain John Davis had referred to as the Furious Overfall (now Hudson Strait) separates Baffin Island from the mainland of northern Quebec. The strait has high tides, fast currents, and, during the brief summer navigation season, much heavy, drifting ice. The coast of southern Baffin Island is a rugged maze of high cliffs, deep inlets, large rocks, and rafted ice pushing tight against the shores. The opposite coast, to the west of Ungava Bay and now part of Quebec, is a mix of bays, river mouths, high lands, and many rugged offshore islands.

Off the south coast of Greenland, *Discovery* would have joined a westbound surface current. Two-thirds of the way across the southern end of Davis Strait, that current is collected by a strong southbound flow streaming from northern Baffin Island and extending far down the coast of Labrador. It is also joined by the considerable outflow from Hudson Strait. These combined currents, along with powerful tides, icebergs, and drifting ice floes, would prove an unprecedented challenge to *Discovery* and its crew.

CHAPTER

7

Drifting Ice, Cold Fogs, and a Hint of Mutiny

RESOLUTION ISLAND STANDS LIKE A sentinel off the southeastern tip of Baffin Island. Along with the much smaller Button Islands, forty-five miles to the south and off the northern extremity of the Labrador coast, Resolution guards the entrance to the turmoil of Hudson Strait.

The Canadian government's *Sailing Directions: Arctic Canada* warns, "The greatest tidal range in the Canadian Arctic is found in the eastern part of Hudson Strait. At Leaf Basin in Ungava Bay [off the mouth of the Leaf River, in the southwest corner of Ungava Bay], a maximum spring range of 14.8 m (48.5 ft.) has been recorded." Of course, none of this important tidal and current flow information was available in Hudson's time.

Discovery passed Resolution Island and entered the strait around June 25. The ship was swept westward along the rocky southern shore of Baffin Island. The currents in the strait were more than Hudson's crew could handle at first. They soon found their ship changing direction and being carried south across the strait into the huge, funnel-shaped Ungava Bay. The crew saw an iceberg split in two and overturn, causing some of the men to fear for their lives. Ice floes littered the sea, many much larger than *Discovery*. Crashing into and rafting over each other, they slammed into the sheer cliffs of Akpatok Island and shattered into smaller though still deadly blocks.

The ice and *Discovery* were at the mercy of the currents and tides. Dragged deep into the bay and threatened with being wrecked on Akpatok, the ship would be released into the strait only to be recaptured and swept back into the bay. Another potential hazard appeared: polar bears were seen on some of the floes and bergs. The crew commented on the bears jumping off the ice into the water. Fortunately, they stayed away from the ship.

While in the recesses of Ungava Bay, Hudson allowed his own fears to show, at least to Abacuck Prickett, who wrote, "Here our Master was in despair, and, (as he told me after) he thought he should never have got out of this ice, but there have perished."

The threat of mutiny seems to have surfaced around this time. Hudson did not mention it, but Prickett alluded to it

A sailing ship nears a towering iceberg and walruses at the entrance to Hudson Strait. From a watercolour by George Back.

LIBRARY AND ARCHIVES CANADA 1979-49-1

with the following revelation: "Therefore he brought forth his card [navigation chart], and showed all the company, that he had sailed farther west in the strait than any other Englishman had, and left it to their choice whether they would proceed any farther; yea or nay."

Prickett continued with the men's responses: "Some were of one mind, and some of another, some wishing themselves at home, and some not caring where, so [long as] they were out of the ice." Then came the telling words "But there were some who then spoke words, which were remembered a great while after."

The men argued back and forth. Hudson, it becomes obvious, had lost control of them by then, at least for the moment. One man told Hudson that if he had a hundred pounds, he would give ninety of that to be at home. The carpenter, Philip Staffe, disagreed. He let everyone know whose side he was on when he announced that if he had a hundred pounds, he would not give ten of them under any conditions to be anywhere else.

Prickett concludes the story of the discord with, "After many words to no purpose . . . the men had to go back to work to get the ship out of danger." The threat of mutiny was over for the moment but would rear its ugly head again.

After being trapped by the ice and unruly currents in Ungava Bay, *Discovery* finally broke free and crawled along the southern coast of the strait. For days the ship fought her way against the drifting ice. When it was too thick to push through, Hudson anchored *Discovery* to the floes and waited for a break to set his ship free again. With constant changes of direction and many frights from the encroaching ice, they eventually reached a high cape that Hudson named for one of his benefactors (Cape Wolstenholme). Just to the west was an island, which he later named for Sir Dudley Digges.

Off Cape Wolstenholme, Hudson sent one of the ship's boats ashore with Prickett, Staffe, and a few others. Their instructions were to explore the land to the west, northwest, and southwest. The weather proved unfriendly and pelted them with rain while deafening them with thunder and scaring them with lightning. Ignoring the storm as much as possible, they climbed to the highest point of land. There, on a grassy plain, they saw a herd of caribou (Prickett called them deer) but could not get close enough to shoot any. Near a waterfall they found a breeding ground of waterfowl and, as Prickett noted, "the best grass that I had seen since we came from England."

They also discovered large areas of sorrel and scurvy-grass, both useful additions to a ship's pantry. Soon after, they were surprised to find they were not the only human beings in the area. They came upon mysterious stone structures, similar to cairns, and hanging from one were strings of dead fowl. Before they could explore farther, they were recalled to *Discovery* by musket fire. Fog was rolling in, and Hudson had no wish to lose men onshore.

The northwest passage Hudson was looking for in this location was actually the impossible route denied Martin Frobisher thirty-two years earlier. The true entry to the modern-day Northwest Passage from the east is at Lancaster Sound, between northern Baffin Island and Devon Island, hundreds of nautical miles north from where Hudson was exploring. That access point would not be discovered for another 250 years. Meanwhile, Hudson's search for the elusive passage in the strait would prove as frustrating as Frobisher's and far more daunting.

In early September, Hudson belatedly decided to display his authority by bringing up the subject of the mutinous talk in Ungava Bay a few weeks before. Prickett wrote, "Our Master took occasion to revive old matter, and to displace Robert Juet from being his Mate, and the Bo'sun from his place for words spoken in the first great bay of ice."

Thomas Woodhouse, a young mathematician serving as a common seaman, also wrote an account of these proceedings. The few pages under his name were found, presumably at the end of the voyage, tucked away in his desk on the ship. Woodhouse was more specific about the event than was Prickett. Woodhouse wrote that the discussion, or trial, was held after dinner in front of the ship's company on September 10, 1610, at Juet's request. Juet wanted an apology for what he considered to be certain verbal abuses and slanders against his name. Some of the crew took this opportunity to speak against him in public.

Bennett Matthews testified that Juet had threatened to turn the ship for England after they had left Iceland, and that he had made the threat in front of many of the crew. If true, that threat equated to mutiny. Matthews also accused Juet of speaking of blood to be shed on board.

Philip Staffe and Arnold Ludlowe had similar accusations against Juet. They swore on the Bible that Juet had "persuaded them to keep muskets charged, and swords ready in their cabins, for they should be charged with shot before the voyage was over."

A fourth accusation was that Juet had used words suggesting mutiny, discouragement, and slander when the ship was caught in the ice in Ungava Bay.

Another captain would have had Juet flogged or hanged from the yardarm for such talk. Hudson showed his weakness by accepting the accusations and passing a mild judgement. He demoted Juet from mate to ordinary seaman. In his place, Hudson appointed Robert Bylot to be second-in-command. Francis Clements was demoted also, from bosun to ordinary seaman, probably because he supported Juet, and was replaced by William Wilson (Thomas Woodhouse did not trust William Wilson; he suggested that Wilson was a sneak). In another sign of weakness, Hudson promised Juet and Clements that with good behaviour and honest work, their sins would be forgotten in time.

Neither Juet nor Clements would have been happy about losing their status as ship's officers. (For Juet, having to take orders from a subordinate such as Bylot would have been especially galling.) Nor would Juet and Clements have been happy about the corresponding loss in pay.

Despite his officer status as second-in-command for the voyage up to that time, it is obvious that Juet had built a reputation as a malcontent. Now, with both him and Clements reduced in rank, the atmosphere on board must have been as volatile as a powder keg with a lighted fuse.

The Arctic winds increased and, as if mocking Hudson's often indecisive nature, sent *Discovery* on an erratic course. She sailed north and then south and then to the north again, where she found shoal water. Hudson decided to rest at anchor until the foul weather improved. For eight days they stood in seven or eight fathoms of water in a bay. Not once during that time did the winds relent enough for the crew to haul anchor. On the eighth day, as the winds began to decrease, Hudson ordered the anchor up. Some of the crew disagreed with the decision and said so; Captain Hudson was losing control again.

Getting the anchor up should have been a routine task. Sailors manned the capstan wheel and turned it in circles until the anchor came clear of the sea. On this occasion, though, something went wrong. The anchor came up as it should, but then a sudden surge of waves or a natural swell rocked the ship violently, and the men were thrown from the capstan. With nothing to stop it, the anchor dropped. Philip Staffe was quick to take action. He chopped through the fast-running cable with his axe to prevent the loss of all but a short portion of it. The anchor, free from restraint, went to the seabed, from where it could not be retrieved. A few of the men working the capstan were injured when the wave hit. Prickett's account suggested that he, too, was hurt but did not say to what degree.

The ship now sailed south and at times southwest over the next few days. The sea changed colour. Prickett recorded two distinct shades, one black and the other almost white, over a depth of sixteen or seventeen fathoms. This was almost certainly where the ship crossed from Hudson Bay into James Bay. As darkness fell, Hudson ordered the topsail taken in and let the ship run before the wind under mainsail and foresail. Soundings showed the depth under the keel to be getting shallower. At five fathoms, Hudson turned the ship to the east, looking for deeper water. With more space under the keel, he turned south again, then southwest, and so to anchor in a bay to the west.

A handful of men went ashore in a small boat. The seabed shallowed rapidly, and the men had to get out and walk a long distance in ankle-deep water and mud, but they made it to land. On the shore they found human footprints. They also found ducks and dry wood, taking some of both back to *Discovery*.

From the anchorage, rocks were visible to the north and the south; Prickett noted that they were covered at high tide. He also noted that the tide ran strong. At midnight, Hudson weighed anchor, intending to take *Discovery* out of the bay the way she had come in. Philip Staffe, the carpenter, who was normally on his captain's side, approached Hudson and warned him that the course he had set would take the ship onto the rocks. Hudson was convinced that he was past the danger and said so. A few minutes later, Staffe's judgement was shown to be correct—*Discovery* ran up on the rocks and was stuck there for a full twelve hours. She came off eventually, as Prickett recorded, "by the Grace of God . . . unhurt, though not unscarred."

The crew's confidence in their captain had taken another knock, but they continued with their duties. Once off the rocks, *Discovery* sailed east, crossing to the opposite shore of James Bay. By this time the nights were getting longer, and the cold was felt increasingly by the men. Hudson decided to look for a safe place in which to shelter for the coming winter.

Discovery had left England in April with enough food for eight months. By November, Prickett wrote, six months' worth of provisions remained stored on board. (In that estimate, he might have been a trifle optimistic.) Even so, all on board recognized the need to hunt for birds and any other game that came within range whenever possible in order to supplement the food stocks. There is a suggestion in Prickett's report that he might have sensed that the captain was hoarding food for his own use. He wrote, "If our Master would have had more, he might have had it at home and in other places." It was certainly not unknown for sea captains to siphon off some of the food provided to the ship to leave with their families during the long months of separation. Hudson could have been guilty of such an act.

Now that the decision had been made to spend the winter where they were, Hudson ordered the remaining food to be strictly rationed. He also gave the men an incentive to hunt by offering a reward for the men who brought in red meat, fish, or fowl.

The weeks passed, and winter loomed; the air chilled and the first snow fell. With it, the sea temperature dropped and the waters of the bay began to freeze. James Bay is 120 miles wide and 280 miles long. Its southern extremity touches latitude 51° north. London, England, is actually farther north, but although James Bay and parts of England share the same latitude, there the similarities end. Hudson might have expected to encounter similar weather to that of his home country; if so, he was far off track. James Bay is subject to an Arctic climate, far worse than anything experienced in England. It suffers mighty storms and blizzards and in winter is completely covered by ice.

James Bay is fed by dozens of freshwater rivers on both its east and west sides. Due to this constant flow, its own waters are diluted and become brackish rather than salty; consequently, the bay freezes over earlier than the much bigger and more saline Hudson Bay, and it stays frozen for about six months each year. Soon, with no escape to the north through the pack ice, Hudson had no alternative but to find somewhere to beach *Discovery* and make a haven for the winter. There would be no sitting in front of home fires at Christmas 1610 for this ship's crew.

The western and southwestern shores were too shallow for a safe moorage, and the low-lying countryside was little more than peat bog for some distance inland. By mid-November, Hudson had secured his ship close to the rocky southeastern shore of James Bay, which he deemed to be the safest location. (This is believed to have been in the vicinity of today's Rupert Bay.) The waters soon froze around the hull, and the ship was trapped for the winter. Its prison of ice would not begin to melt for many months, until the sun returned to spread warmth over the surrounding land. Life would be hard, but the crew, like Prickett, believed they had enough food on board to keep them all alive for the winter. They were wrong: they would need substantial additional rations to survive.

In mid-November, the gunner, John Williams, died. The reason for his death was never recorded, but it created tension among the crew. Prickett noted the death with a shot at the captain and a look into the future. This latter part of his report was obviously written after he returned to England: "God pardon the Master's uncharitable dealing with this man [John Williams]. Now for that I am come to speak of him [John Williams], out of whose ashes (as it were) that unhappy deed grew which brought a scandal upon all that are returned home, and upon the action itself, the multitude (like the dog) running after the stone, but not at the caster: therefore, not to wrong the living, nor slander the dead, I will (by the leave of God) deliver the truth as near as I can."

Here in his journal, or report, after his mention of John Williams, Prickett refers back to early on in the voyage when Henry Greene came on board—and even before that. Prickett wrote that Greene was born in Kent of respectable parents. He was educated but became a wanton young man who lost the confidence of his friends and parents due to his lifestyle. Henry Hudson had taken him to live in his own house with his family and planned to take him to sea with him because, Prickett said, Greene could write. Greene, however, would not be listed on the ship's roster, nor would he receive any pay. He came aboard as a visitor near Gravesend and should have left the ship at Harwich with the other visitor who had come aboard briefly.

With these revelations, it appears that Prickett was attempting to establish a basis for the crew's distrust of their captain and of Henry Greene. He continued these late entries to his journal with the story of the fight between Greene and Wilson in Iceland.

Prickett had reported the incident to Hudson, who, he said, told him to let it alone because "the surgeon had a tongue that would wrong the best friend he had."

Prickett then took issue with Juet in his report: "But Robert Juet would needs burn his fingers in the embers and told the carpenter a long tale (when he was drunk) that Hudson had brought Greene on board to spy on other members of the crew."

All of this was leading up to Prickett's account of another source of discontentment on board the unhappy ship. When a sailor died at sea, his possessions were offered to other crew members for the best price. Williams, the gunner, had owned a cloak of grey cloth. Greene admired the garment and asked Hudson if he could have it—without paying for it. Hudson had agreed that when the time came for the sale, the cloak should go to Greene and to no other. A subsequent event caused Hudson to reverse his decision, and so, once again, the captain's lack of resolution would cause trouble.

CHAPTER

8

A Winter in the Ice

WITH THE SHIP AS SECURE as it could be in its precarious wilderness position, Hudson set the crew to work building a house on the shore. The task gave the men something new to think about while they prepared for a savage winter, but even this relatively simple task caused dissension. Ship's carpenter Philip Staffe, who had been a conscientious, law-abiding sailor until then, argued against building the house and refused to have anything to do with it. Despite Hudson's wrath, which was intense enough that he struck Staffe and called him foul names, the latter would not give in. He said he was not a house carpenter. Other crew members went ashore and built the house in Staffe's place. Staffe was not punished for his refusal to follow orders.

Soon after, Staffe went ashore to hunt. Hudson's rule was that no man should wander off alone: there must always be two together, one with a loaded musket, the other with a pike. Hudson did not specify that certain men should not go ashore together, but because of his earlier clash with Staffe, he got angry with Greene when the latter accompanied Staffe. In consequence, Hudson told Robert Bylot he could have the gunner's cloak. The scene was set for another bitter confrontation—again caused by Hudson's exceptional attitude to his crews.

When Greene returned to the ship and saw Bylot with the cloak, he complained to Hudson. The captain replied with insults against Greene's personality and manner. Hudson also told Greene he would not receive any wages if he did not do as the captain said. Prickett wrote of Greene's reaction, "You shall see how the devil out of this so wrought with Greene, that he did the Master what mischief he could in seeking to discredit him, and to thrust him and many other honest men out of the ship in the end." With that, Prickett announced to any prospective readers of his journal that Henry Greene had been the instigator of the mutiny that would soon play out in James Bay.

Prickett had little more to say on that subject, except for a weak excuse that revealed no specific details: "To speak of all our trouble in this time of winter (which was so cold as it lamed the most of our company, and myself do yet feel it) would be too tedious."

Prickett writes that during the early winter, the men shot partridges (probably ptarmigan), ducks, and geese by the hundreds as the birds migrated south. When the flocks had gone and other food supplies ran low, the hungry men resorted to eating anything that moved, including frogs.

Little is really known of that winter, other than that it was a harsh experience for all on board *Discovery.* Prickett makes no mention of the house the crew built on the shore being used. In fact, he only saw one event as especially important. Thomas Woodhouse had brought some plant buds back to the ship after an excursion through the woods. The bud, Woodhouse showed, was filled with a turpentine-like substance, which he boiled in water and made into a palatable drink. It was also used as the main ingredient in a poultice and applied to aches and pains on the body. Prickett, who suffered much, said, "I received great and present ease of my pain."

Apart from that, no one—not even Prickett—thought to record the daily happenings while they were trapped in the ice. Undoubtedly, they were too busy trying to stay alive until spring arrived. When the ice did begin its breakup, the beleaguered crew received a surprise visitor. A Native man came to the ship alone sometime around the end of May 1611. He was almost certainly from the Cree Nation.

Hudson asked the crew to hand in their knives and hatchets as gifts to the Native, but only a few of them complied with the request. Hudson gave the man a few presents of his own, hoping for an opportunity to trade later. The

Native left but returned the next day hauling a sledge loaded with two beaver pelts and two deerskins. Hudson proved to be a hard bargainer in this case, and the Native received less than he had hoped for his skins. He did indicate that others lived in the vicinity, to the north and south. He also led Hudson to believe he would return soon, but he never did, and no other Native people showed themselves.

The birds were long gone and would not return for some weeks, but under the ice, the sea was rich in nourishment. As the ice began to break up, Hudson sent seven men out in the shallop with a large net to catch fish. The expedition proved successful, and they returned carrying some five hundred fish—most about the size of a herring, and some that Prickett referred to as trout. There was certainly enough in the net to feed all on board for many days. They must have run into a few passing shoals of various types of fish on that occasion: although the nets were cast again on subsequent days, that generous haul was never repeated.

The expanses of open water and the apparent abundance of fish prompted Greene and William Wilson, with a couple of others, to think about leaving the ship and fending for themselves. According to Prickett, they planned to take the shallop and the large fishing net. The captain ruined their plans when he took the boat himself and, with a few loyal men, sailed south to search for Native villages. While they were gone, the rest of the crew were ordered to fill the freshwater casks, take on board extra ballast, and generally make the ship ready for sea.

Despite seeing evidence, as he sailed slowly along the coast, of cooking fires and forest fires he believed Native people had set, Hudson was unable to meet or even see anyone. Disappointed after being away for a week or more, he returned to *Discovery*.

In the captain's absence, the crew had not been idle. In accordance with his instructions, they had prepared *Discovery* to break out of its icy mooring. They should have been happy at the prospect of getting out of the bay and back to sea, and the thought of possibly going home, but trouble was again astir.

Prickett's journal shows that Captain Hudson was at this point a worried man. On his return from his unprofitable voyage looking for Native people, he made three curious decisions. First he demoted Robert Bylot from his position as mate and replaced him with John King. Then he had all the bread removed from the ship's stores and divided equally among all on board; this gave each man about one pound of bread. He had also prepared what Prickett called "a bill of Return," which was for each man to show (to authorities) should the ship make it safely home. Prickett said Hudson wept as he gave these to them. This document, similar in content to the one Hudson had given his crew on *Hopewell* while on his second Arctic voyage, was, it appears, a feeble attempt to forestall yet another mutiny.

For some crewmen, the bread did not last long; they devoured it quickly and were soon hungry again. Some fish was left, but that store was dwindling fast. The day the bread was handed out, a few men went fishing again and brought in about eighty small fish.

Discovery sailed out of James Bay and anchored in the huge bay to the north (Hudson Bay). There, Hudson repeated the mistake of dividing up what was believed to be all that was left of the food. He shared out five large rounds of cheese among the men, which gave them about three and a half pounds each—enough to last each of them a week or more if they were careful with it.

When the winds allowed, *Discovery* set sail for the northwest. That was not the most direct course to England, and the crew knew it. Hudson was once again setting off to search for a northwest passage. The tempers of some in the crew began to boil. They all wanted to go home, not spend another winter trapped in ice in a foreign land. On the evening of Monday, June 18, 1611, the ship encountered drifting ice. The next morning, with the wind against them, Prickett noted that the ship stayed put in sight of land. Day after day the men waited for the wind to change direction. Captain Hudson used part of that enforced wait to once more antagonize his crew.

He ordered Nicholas Simms, the ship's boy, to open the personal chests of all crewmen and take out any bread or other food stored there. At the end of his search, the boy delivered a large bag containing thirty cakes of bread to the captain. For some of the crew, it was the final insult.

CHAPTER

9

Mutiny On the Bay

ON SATURDAY, JUNE 20, HENRY GREENE and William Wilson approached Abacuck Prickett and told him they and some other crew members intended to remove Henry Hudson from command and then take over the ship. They planned to put the captain, his son John, and some sick and injured men into the shallop and cast them adrift to fend for themselves. They warned that any who were against Greene and his followers would be added to the shallop's passenger list.

Prickett cautioned Wilson and Greene that the consequences would be extreme. Most of the men had wives and children at home. If they went through with the mutiny, they could never return home—unless they wanted to be hanged. They would be forever exiled from their native country and from their families.

"Don't you understand? What you are proposing is mutiny, and that is a hanging offence. You'll be dancing from the gallows as soon as you get home," Prickett warned.

"Hold your tongue, Prickett," replied Greene. "I would rather be hanged at home than starved abroad."

In his later description of the mutiny, the reasons Prickett gave for this rebellious act were that there was only enough food to last a few days, and the captain had shown he cared little for his crew. The mutineers had vowed to end Hudson's rule and either get home or die in the attempt.

Greene refused to listen to Prickett's warnings, telling him to mind his own business. Greene and Wilson also told Prickett that they meant him no harm. If he wished, he could stay aboard *Discovery* and return home with them. Prickett thanked them for the thought but declined. Greene replied that Prickett must then join the captain and the sick men in the shallop and take his chances. Prickett accepted his fate, putting his trust in God.

Greene lost his temper at Prickett's mild acceptance of the situation and stormed away for a while, leaving Wilson and Prickett alone. When he returned, he showed his anxiety and, perhaps, his paranoia, by demanding to know what they had talked about in his absence. Wilson explained that Prickett had simply reiterated the legal implications of the impending mutiny. In an effort to delay the crime, Prickett asked for a day or two to discuss the situation of food with the captain and try to make peace between the master and crew. Greene, however, was out for blood. He wanted revenge on Henry Hudson and was determined to have it. Nothing Prickett could say would sway him from his chosen course. Greene also decided to keep Prickett on board *Discovery* rather than casting him adrift with the captain, because Prickett was one of the few who could read and write.

Greene took Prickett's Bible, laid his hand on it, and swore he would not harm any man aboard. What he was about to do, he said, was for the good of the voyage and for no other reason. He then said all others should swear the same. William Wilson followed him. Greene left Prickett then, but soon Robert Juet arrived. He, Prickett said, "was worse than Henry Greene. He swore that he would justify this deed when he got home." One by one and two by two, the other mutineers came by to swear on Prickett's Bible. The oath they swore was blasphemous and contradictory to the actions they were about to take. Only Prickett seemed to understand that fact. He must have administered the oath, because, he said, he wrote the oath as it was spoken, without adding or taking anything away.

The oath read, "You shall swear truth to God, your prince and country: you shall do nothing, but to the glory of God and the good of the action in hand, and harm to no man."

Prickett was well aware that by being involved in these proceedings, he was setting himself up for an accusation of mutiny by association if he should survive to voyage home. He knew that if he were found guilty, he would hang with the rest of the mutineers.

Robert Juet and Hudson's erstwhile friend Henry Greene, plus a handful of sailors, were about to make the ultimate challenge to the captain's authority. Whether they fully understood it or not, their actions were in fact punishable by hanging—and there was no time limit. Once word of the mutiny reached England, the perpetrators would be hunted down on land or sea. That night, in spite of Prickett's entreaties, the plan to remove the captain moved one stage closer to its conclusion.

When Prickett asked who else would be cast adrift in the shallop, Greene told him it would be the carpenter (Philip Staffe), the first mate (John King), and the sick and lame men. John King was to be abandoned because the captain had made him mate after demoting Robert Bylot when they were leaving their wintering anchorage in James Bay. King, Prickett claimed, could neither read nor write and therefore was useless in that position. Here, in his journal, Prickett makes the point that the mutineers believed Hudson had engineered the change of mate deliberately so that only he, the captain, would know what went into the log and where the ship was going. Prickett said Hudson had demanded the men hand over any and all writing materials so that no one but he could report on the voyage. Prickett did not explain how he came to retain his own writing materials (and, evidently, he was not the only one to hide quills, ink, and paper, as Thomas Woodhouse's few paragraphs, later discovered, attest).

Well aware that the carpenter was a useful man to have aboard ship, especially with a long, hard voyage ahead of them, Prickett begged Greene and Juet to allow Philip Staffe to remain on board, but his plea was ignored.

As the mutineers rested before going into action, Greene spent some time with Hudson in the master's cabin, playing the violin to keep him occupied. As they contemplated what they planned to do at daybreak, the rest of the mutineers, and the innocent members of the crew, were scattered about the ship in their customary off-duty positions. To those not yet apprised of the situation, all appeared normal.

Five of the crew suffered from ailments. The cooper, Sylvanus Bond, was lame, as was Syracke Fanning. Thomas Woodhouse was sick—possibly from scurvy. Michael Butt and Adrian Moore had been on the sick list since the loss of the anchor in October 1610, probably having suffered leg or arm injuries at that time. Unknown to them, most of these men were condemned to be cast adrift with the captain.

At sunrise on June 22, the mutineers went to work. First they had to take care of those few men loyal to Hudson. The cook locked John King in the hold. Greene engaged Philip Staffe in conversation with a third man.

Someone else made sure John, the captain's son, could not sound the alarm. Meanwhile, there was the captain to take care of. Henry Hudson was in his cabin, half-asleep, when he heard a noise outside.

"Captain. Captain," a rough voice called. Hudson rolled off his bunk, opened the cabin door, and stepped out. Facing him were Bennett Matthews, the ship's cook, and John Thomas, an ordinary seaman. Before he could assess the situation, Hudson was grabbed from behind by William Wilson's huge hands and forced to the deck, where his arms were trussed behind him with rope.

"What is the meaning of this outrage?" demanded Hudson as he struggled against his captors.

"You'll find out soon enough once you are in the shallop," came Wilson's surly answer.

Meanwhile, loyal crew member John King had gone to the hold and was shut in before he could escape. Trapped there, he was not prepared to give up easily. He found a sword, and when Robert Juet came into the hold to reason with him, trying to persuade him to join the uprising, King would have none of it and attacked Juet with the sword. Had Juet not called for help and received the assistance of two or three fellow mutineers, King would almost certainly have killed the mate and created havoc when he got free. It wasn't to be. King was subdued by an overwhelming force, taken up on deck, and condemned to the same fate as his captain. Young John Hudson was also overpowered.

After Captain Hudson, John Hudson, John King, Michael Butt, Syracke Fanning, Arnold Ludlowe, Adrian Moore, and Thomas Woodhouse were put into the shallop on Greene's order, Hudson called out to Prickett that Juet was responsible for the mutiny and would overthrow them all. Prickett shouted back that Hudson was wrong. "Nay," he called, "not Juet, but that villain Henry Greene."

Philip Staffe was still on board *Discovery* and free of any restraints. When the mutineers invited him to join them, he refused, saying he would not stay on the ship unless they forced him to do so. Greene told him to get over the side and board the shallop. Staffe said he would but not until he had collected his tools, which he did; he then joined the captain in the small boat.

In addition to his carpentry tools, Staffe had managed to take with him a musket, powder and shot, a couple of pikes, and an iron pot, plus some basic food supplies. Hudson and his small group were in dire straits, but at least they had a few items with which to defend themselves, if necessary, and, possibly, to help them hunt for fresh meat on land.

Both the *Discovery* and the shallop were still partly confined by ice. The smaller boat was tied to the stern of *Discovery*, towed partway out of the ice jam, and then cast adrift.

Aboard *Discovery*, Henry Greene gave the order to set all sails and make way for open water to the northeast and for England. As the wind filled the ship's canvas, she pulled away, her bowsprit pointing due north, and left the shallop behind.

Hudson's loyal crew managed to quickly rig a small sail. That, combined with a few men at the oars, moved the shallop forward in pursuit of the ship.

On *Discovery*, the most unruly men were already ransacking the ship, searching for food, clothing, and anything else of value. The men found a store of food in the hold, including one and a half containers of meal, two firkins of butter, twenty-seven pieces of salt pork, and half a bushel of peas. In the captain's cabin they found additional treasures: two hundred biscuit cakes, a peck of meal, and a barrel of beer. While they were searching the ship, the other mutineers had taken in the topsail and were holding a slow course under foresail alone.

A lookout on deck noticed the shallop slowly catching up to them. He called the alarm, and the crew responded. They shook out the mainsail and topsail and soon left the shallop far behind. No matter how hard the castaways rowed, they had no chance of catching the much faster sailing ship carrying the thirteen mutineers. Soon *Discovery*'s topmasts disappeared over the horizon. Captain Henry Hudson and his handful of loyal crew were completely alone on a dangerous sea bordered by a hostile, desolate land. Their fate would now rest on their ability to fend for themselves.

Captain Henry Hudson and his son, John, cast adrift with a handful of loyal crew members. From an original painting by John Collier.

LIBRARY AND ARCHIVES CANADA C-002061

Close to the eastern shore, the mutineers changed course for the west until they saw an island. Its location is unknown, but it could have been one of the Belcher Islands. *Discovery* anchored in sixteen or seventeen fathoms while a small boat went ashore. The ship could not approach closer due to the rocks along the coastline. Michael Perse shot two large birds, and he and his companions collected a bundle of cockle grass, which, they knew from experience, was nutritious and could help stave off the dreaded scurvy.

Discovery remained at anchor for the night and part of the next day. To the relief of many on board, there was no sign of Hudson's shallop. At this time, Greene approached Prickett and asked him to move into the captain's cabin and take care of everything in there, presumably to prevent the theft of Hudson's belongings by other crew members. Despite Abacuck Prickett's protestations that Robert Juet was far more suited to that task, he eventually agreed to the request.

Without Henry Hudson on board, no leader became apparent at first. The three strongest characters were Henry Greene, Robert Juet, and Robert Bylot. The last had apparently not taken any active part in the mutiny. When they left the island behind, Juet, without explaining why, wanted to sail to the northwest. Bylot spoke up for a northeasterly course, which was more in the direction of home, and his wishes were followed. For a while the ship sailed parallel to the eastern shore of the great bay. A gale blew in, and with it came ice. Soon *Discovery* was once again beset. For fourteen anxious days, the mutineers were trapped in the worst ice they had ever encountered, wrote Prickett. As the ice relented and fractures appeared, opening up leads wide enough for the ship, Juet again wanted to sail northwest. Again Bylot contradicted him and recommended the northeast. Bylot's course was chosen once more, and *Discovery* cruised carefully along the coast until she was clear of the ice.

Off a group of four islands, the wind failed and the ship drifted back to the northernmost pair and anchored between them. A reconnaissance of the islands showed no signs of fresh meat, but the shore party did bring back more cockle grass.

While they were at anchor, Henry Greene began to harass Abacuck Prickett, accusing him of stealing many of the captain's belongings—items which, Prickett maintained, Greene had actually stolen. Prickett's narrative shows that by this time, Henry Greene had been accepted as the new captain of the ship. When the men began to talk of the dangers of returning to England, Greene pledged to keep the ship at sea until they had an assurance in writing from the king of England that they would come to no harm in their homeland.

Neither Bylot nor Juet knew exactly where they were, and Greene and the rest of the crew were no wiser. The ship sailed north, and the lookouts saw nothing they recognized. Some argued to go south again, believing the ship had already passed the known landmarks, but Bylot persevered in his own navigation. Prickett now said he believed they were near Cape Wolstenholme; Juet disagreed. Prickett turned out to be correct. Within a few days, the cape was in sight, and the men smiled with relief. At last they were in familiar seas.

Close to the cape, *Discovery* ran aground and was held fast on a rock on an ebb tide for eight or nine harrowing hours. The flood took them off again without damage, and they were able to anchor close to shore. Although the wind was blowing off the land, some men rowed one of the ship's boats ashore to hunt for fowl. They were disappointed: no ducks or geese were seen, but they did see many gulls and shot about thirty of them for the cooking pot before returning to the ship as night fell.

Discovery by then was close to the southwestern end of Hudson Strait. On the outbound journey the previous year, the crew had collected a store of fowl at a breeding site near there. Natives had stored the birds in stone cairns to keep out scavengers and to preserve them from the elements. Now the crew could not find it. They knew of another breeding ground on Cape Digges, so they turned toward that high island in the ship's boat. To the surprise of all on board, seven boats carrying Native people came out to meet them.

No one in *Discovery*'s crew was inclined to trust the Natives, but they did need their help in locating the fowl they sought. To avoid conflict, both sides took a hostage.

One of the Englishmen boarded a Native boat, and one of the Natives boarded *Discovery*'s small boat. Together the boats went ashore, where the Natives had put up their tents. The English hostage was placed in a tent under guard. The Native hunters then took the foreigners to the breeding ground and showed them how they caught the big birds: using a long pole equipped with a noose on the end, they would snare a bird's neck and pull it from its perch on the rocks. In return, the Englishmen showed their more efficient, though noisier, method of hunting. One blast from a musket downed seven or more birds at a time.

After a small amount of trading at the tent village, the hostages were reexchanged and the Englishmen went back to their ship. They planned to return the following day, when the Natives (as they had explained using sign language) would have fresh venison to trade. Accordingly, Greene, Prickett, and four other men went ashore again the next day. Having been greeted in friendly fashion the day before, they went unarmed except for the daggers all seamen wore on their belts. Greene also carried a pike with a shortened staff. None of the Natives appeared to be armed either.

The peaceful trading did not last long. Without warning, a Native attacked Prickett, who was sitting in the boat. The knife attack gave Prickett wounds in his arm, chest, and thigh. Despite this, he managed to overpower his assailant and turn the knife against him, stabbing him in the chest before cutting his throat.

Sailing ships and Inuit kayaks near the Savage Islands in Hudson Strait. From a watercolour by George Back.

LIBRARY AND ARCHIVES CANADA C-040364

The men onshore had no chance to help their shipmate because they too were set upon by a group of Natives. Prickett wrote of the scene, "John Thomas and William Wilson had their bowels cut, and Michael Perse and Henry Greene being mortally wounded, came tumbling into the boat together." Andrew Motter ran across the rocks, dived into the sea, and swam to the boat, which was still against the shore. Michael Perse grabbed Motter's shirt and hauled him aboard.

The bloody melee continued, with Natives attacking the boat from all sides and the Englishmen doing their best to defend themselves and their wounded. Prickett pushed the boat out and managed to turn it as the Natives shot at them with bows and arrows. Prickett took one arrow in the back. Henry Greene died of his wounds in the boat. Michael Perse suffered numerous wounds, as did most of the others. Perse and Motter rowed hard to get the boat out of range, until Perse fainted from the severity of his wounds. Motter stood up in the bow and waved to the ship to come and help them.

Without ceremony, Henry Greene's body was pushed overboard. Andrew Motter and William Wilson died that day, too, Wilson "swearing and cursing in a most dreadful manner." Michael Perse lived another two days before he succumbed to his wounds. Of the original thirteen mutineers, only Juet, Bylot, the wounded Prickett, and a handful of sick and lame men were left alive. Somehow, they had to sail their ship the length of Hudson Strait and the vast width of the Atlantic Ocean to reach home. They also had to find ways to feed themselves.

It seems Juet now took command of the ship. As the eldest, the former first mate, and the most experienced sailor on board, it was perhaps fitting that he should do so. He was ably assisted in his new role by the stalwart Robert Bylot, who would soon prove his worth as a navigator.

Before beginning the long voyage to the east, *Discovery* sailed back and forth at the western end of Hudson Strait because there was nowhere safe for them to anchor. Men went ashore, in spite of the danger from Natives, and collected about two hundred fowl. Then, with food on board, they sailed east. The wind soon stopped them and drove the ship back toward the cape. Taking another risk, some went ashore again and killed another hundred birds for the cooking pot.

As soon as the wind veered to blow from the west, Juet sailed *Discovery* along the north side of the strait, following the rugged south shore of Baffin Island. The wind must have been substantial and steady, because the sea current on the north side of the strait sets mostly to the west. After one night at anchor, the ship continued to the islands guarding the eastern entrance to the strait. There, *Discovery* almost came to grief by running up on Resolution Island's rocks, which were shrouded in thick fog.

Once clear of the land and out in Davis Strait, *Discovery* set course for Desolation Island, off Greenland's east coast. From there, the British Isles should have been their next landfall. The return journey, however, would not be easy. The wind changed to blow hard from the east. Although Robert Juet was nominally in command, he did not have all the powers of a ship's captain. He suggested they use the wind to sail toward Newfoundland, where they should meet fellow countrymen or at least find regular food. *Discovery* sailed southwest and then west close to latitude 57° north—a course that would have carried them to one of hundreds of fjords indenting Labrador's central coast.

To Prickett's relief, the wind changed again, veering to blow from the southwest. Prickett wrote, "Then the Master

[Juet] asked me if he should take the benefit of this wind, and shape his course for Ireland. I said it was best to go where we knew corn grew and not to seek it where it was cast away and not to be found."

And so *Discovery* sailed east, out into the North Atlantic, in hopes of reaching Ireland. By this time their stock of ducks and geese was almost exhausted. The crew did the best with what they had, using candle grease to fry what was left of the birds. When the meat was finished, the cook made a broth from the leftover bones. It was not enough to feed men who needed all their strength to handle the ship. To supplement this starvation diet, Juet boiled the birds' feathers. The men even ate candles and any food garbage left over from the birds.

Discovery began to wander from one side of its course to the other as the helmsmen became too weak to steer properly. The sails were left untended, and the sheets, or ropes, broke from lack of care. The ship was in trouble. Robert Juet died, almost certainly of malnutrition. Bylot then took command.

A few days later, the lookout saw land ahead: it was Ireland. Against all odds, they had crossed the Atlantic and were almost home. They stopped for a few days at Berehaven but found the Irish less than friendly and unwilling to help them. Moving on to England, the ship stopped at Plymouth before continuing to its final stop at Gravesend. *Discovery* had been gone sixteen harrowing, tumultuous months.

CHAPTER

10

Discovery's Crew and Captain: What Happened to Them?

CAPTAIN HENRY HUDSON AND HIS small crew of castaways disappeared into history: none were ever seen or heard from again. Cast adrift by his mutinous crew in the southeastern half of Hudson Bay in June 1611, Hudson was accompanied by the following crew members: John Hudson, the captain's teenaged son, who acted as ship's boy and had served aboard all four of his father's expeditions; Philip Staffe, the ship's carpenter, who had remained loyal to his captain, whether he agreed with Hudson's decisions or not (although there were reports of Staffe openly refusing to obey orders, such as the one to build the house on the shore of James Bay, for the most part he had accepted the captain's commands); the loyal John King, who had been promoted to mate after Robert Bylot's demotion; Thomas Woodhouse, the young mathematician; Arnold Ludlowe, who had been injured by the spinning capstan when *Discovery* lost her anchor; Michael Butt, also injured by the spinning capstan; and, finally, loyal crew members Adrian Moore and Syracke Fanning.

Robert Juet, sometime first mate, sailed with Henry Hudson on three expeditionary voyages. Despite that, the two men had never got along. Juet was older than Hudson and an experienced sailor. Certainly guilty of aiding and abetting the *Discovery* mutiny in 1611, Juet was most likely one of the ringleaders. He died at sea of starvation during *Discovery*'s homeward voyage after the mutiny. His body was committed to the Atlantic Ocean somewhere to the west of Ireland.

Robert Bylot is something of an enigma. Although he did not take part in the mutiny, he did nothing to prevent it or fight against the mutineers. He sailed home with the survivors and should have been hanged by association with the mutiny but was discharged without even a slap on the wrist. He became a respected and knowledgeable Arctic sailor, returning to Hudson Bay in 1612 as navigator under the command of Captain Thomas Button with *Resolution* and *Discovery*. In 1615 he was promoted to captain and, in an ironic twist of fate, was given command of *Discovery*.

He made two more voyages to the Arctic, during which he proved himself to be a highly skilled ice pilot. He died, it is thought, in late 1616 after his return from the second voyage as *Discovery*'s master. Bylot Island, off the north coast of Baffin Island, is named for him.

Abacuck Prickett was not a sailor. He had been placed on board by one of Hudson's benefactors, Sir Dudley Digges, to report on the voyage. Still, he would have been subject to the captain's orders, no matter how unpleasant. Was he a mutineer, or was he an innocent bystander too ineffectual to stand by his captain? History says he was a mutineer—but he got away with it. He returned to Hudson Bay in 1612 as an able seaman, aboard *Discovery* with Robert Bylot and Captain Thomas Button. Prickett and the three other survivors of the 1610–1611 voyage were finally called to account in July 1618. The court of inquiry into the mutiny and almost certain deaths of Captain Hudson and the remainder of the castaways found the mutineers not guilty due to lack of evidence.

Henry Greene, who was certainly one of the ringleaders of the mutiny, was killed by Natives off Digges Island, in the north quadrant of Hudson Bay. His body was put overboard and committed to the deep waters of Hudson Strait.

Nicholas Simms was just a boy, probably of a similar age to John Hudson, and likely would have been dominated by the forceful older crew members. Simms was one of seven original crew members who made it back to England in *Discovery* and somehow avoided the hangman's noose.

Mutineers John Thomas, William Wilson, and Michael Perse were killed by Natives near Digges Island.

Mutineer Bennett Matthews returned to England and disappeared.

Sylvanus Bond and Francis Clements stayed on board *Discovery* with the mutineers and returned to England. Clements then disappeared.

Edward Wilson (no relation to William), the ship's young surgeon, returned to England and was not heard of again.

After mooring *Discovery* at Gravesend, the remaining crew went ashore and vanished. Robert Bylot and Abacuck Prickett travelled to London together and put themselves and their journals at the mercy of the men who had financed the voyage. The justice meted out was unusual: instead of being tried, found guilty of mutiny and murder, and then hanged, Bylot and Prickett were sent back to Hudson Bay with Captain Thomas Button's expedition to search for clues to Henry Hudson's whereabouts and to look for a northwest passage.

Henry Hudson's family never learned what happened to him or his son John. Katherine, Henry's wife, was strong-minded and became known to the directors of the Muscovy Company as "that troublesome and impatient woman."

When Henry and John failed to return on *Discovery* with the remaining members of the original crew, Katherine showed just how tough she was: not for her were the sobbing and wailing of lesser women. Katherine Hudson went after the directors of the Muscovy Company with every resource in her strong mind. She wasn't just looking out for herself—she wanted the company to do something for Richard, her youngest son. The company directors, ever mindful of profit and loss, were reluctant to hand over any money. Instead, they gave Richard a position as a company factor, first at Bantam in Java, later in Japan, and eventually in Bengal. Recognizing that he needed some financial assistance for clothing before he left on a company ship, they scraped up the insignificant sum of five pounds to cover that cost.

Katherine was not impressed by the lack of largesse offered by the company's directors. She continued to lobby them for support, making a considerable nuisance of herself. Katherine knew her own mind. She refused to be put off by the company's parsimonious attitude. Instead, she demanded "a post in the East India trade" for herself. Somehow she won that major battle and travelled to Ahmedabad, India, carrying with her a certain amount of merchandise, such as "quilts and dyes."

After a final clash with the Muscovy Company over who should pay the freight for her goods—the company did, with reluctance—the remarkable Katherine Hudson, widow of the explorer, bowed out of her late husband's story.

Epilogue

WHAT HAPPENED TO HENRY HUDSON and his companions after *Discovery* disappeared over the northern horizon remains a mystery. Possibilities abound, all of which are speculation. There was still much ice in the bay when Hudson and his fellow castaways were set adrift, and, even though it was the third week in June, late spring storms could create extreme danger for a small open boat. Hudson, however, was a professional sailor; he would almost certainly have opted to stay with the shallop and follow the coastline to the north. That, he knew, was the one sure route to the open sea and England, though he would also have known the shallop was not big enough to make the voyage. Had they been able to reach the strait and survive its perils, they could have sailed down the coast of what is now Labrador to Newfoundland and beyond to warmer climes, where they could possibly have encountered European fishing vessels.

Even today, with modern equipment and knowledge, it would be a daunting task—but it could be accomplished, and it could conceivably have been possible in Hudson's time as well. In the summer of 1860, for example, nine men deserted from two American whaling ships in Cumberland Sound on Baffin Island's east coast. They fled south in an open boat less than thirty feet long—not so very different from Hudson's shallop. Those men sailed and rowed nearly fifteen hundred nautical miles to just north of Okak Bay, Labrador, where they were cared for by local Inuit before being handed on to missionaries farther south.

Another alternative, a sensible one, would have been to go ashore, build a communal house shelter, and seek help from Natives, if any could be found and if they would co-operate. Friendly Natives could have assisted them in making their way south and east on rivers and lakes until they reached the St. Lawrence River. Hudson would have known that Jacques Cartier had travelled far up that river some seventy-five years earlier. Ill-equipped as they were and with no survival equipment, the trek to safety would have been a desperate journey of hundreds of miles. But compared to sailing a tiny open boat more than a thousand miles north and then the same distance or more south-southeast along an uncharted coastline, the land option would have made more sense. A major drawback to both journeys, of course, would have been the health of the shallop's crew. When they were cast adrift, four of them were already in poor health due to sickness or injury. With little food between them, the healthy few would soon have shared their companions' miserable state.

Wherever Hudson and his small crew of castaways did go, no records have survived them. They might have starved to death, or the shallop might have been crushed by drifting ice or capsized by waves, and the men on board drowned. Rumours exist of a white boy growing up with Natives on the eastern shores of James Bay in the early decades of the seventeenth century. Could it be true? Could that boy have been John Hudson, Henry's teenaged son? Whether there is truth in those tales is impossible to ever know. Captain Henry Hudson and his small crew of loyal followers rest in unmarked graves, either on the shore or, most likely, on the seabed of Hudson Bay.

It would be another fifty years before Hudson Bay began to fulfill its promise as a commercial waterway. In 1668, *Nonsuch*, chartered by the Company of Adventurers—forerunner of the Hudson's Bay Company—set sail from Gravesend on a trading voyage that took her across the North Atlantic, through Hudson Strait, and south down the length of Hudson Bay to the southern extremity of James Bay. She wintered not far from where *Discovery* had been iced in and returned to England safely the following year with a valuable cargo of furs—and so a new era began.

Although Captain Henry Hudson died in obscurity, his name lives on in many significant North American geographical features, such as Hudson Bay, Hudson Strait, the Hudson River—and the Hudson's Bay Company, the mighty commercial enterprise that helped forge a country. That's some legacy.

Selected Bibliography

Asher, George Michael, ed. *Henry Hudson, The Navigator.* New York: Cambridge University Press, 2010. (This edition first published in 1860. Based on original manuscripts published in 1625—see Purchas, Samuel, below.)

Butts, Edward. *Henry Hudson: New World Voyager.* Toronto: Dundurn, 2009.

Canadian Hydrographic Service. *Pilot of Arctic Canada*, Vol. 1, 2nd ed. Ottawa: Government of Canada, 1970.

Chadwick, Ian. www.ianchadwick.com/hudson

Dalton, Anthony. *Arctic Naturalist: The Life of J. Dewey Soper.* Toronto: Dundurn, 2010.

Department of Fisheries and Oceans. *Sailing Directions: Arctic Canada*, Vol. 1, 3rd ed. Ottawa: Government of Canada, 1982.

Fraser, Robert and William Rannie. *Arctic Adventurer: Grant and the Seduisante.* Lincoln, ON: W.F. Rannie, 1972.

Juet, Robert. *Juet's Journal of Hudson's 1609 Voyage,* from the 1625 edition of *Purchas His Pilgrimes, Vol XIII* by Samuel Purchas. Also from the New Netherland Museum, Albany, NY.

Lambert, R.S. *Mutiny in the Bay.* Toronto: Macmillan, 1966.

Mancall, Peter C. *Fatal Journey: The Final Expedition of Henry Hudson.* New York: Basic Books, 2009.

Nansen, Fridtjof. *Farthest North.* London: Archibald Constable, 1897.

Price, Ray. *The Howling Arctic.* Toronto: Peter Martin Associates, 1970.

Purchas, Samuel. *Hakluytus Posthumus, or Purchas His Pilgrimes, Volume XIII.* Glasgow: James MacLehose, 1907. (Reprint of the 1625 edition.)

Rasky, Frank. *The Polar Voyagers*. Toronto: McGraw-Hill Ryerson, 1976.

Ross, W. Gillies. *Arctic Whalers, Icy Seas*. Toronto: Irwin Publishing, 1985.

Thompson, George Malcolm. *The Search for the Northwest Passage*. New York: Macmillan, 1975.

Tilman, H.W. *Triumph and Tribulation*. Lymington, UK: Nautical Publishing, 1977.

Tyson, Captain George E. *Arctic Experiences Aboard the Doomed Polaris Expedition and Six Months Adrift on an Ice-Floe*. New York: Cooper Square Press, 2002.

Wild, Roland. *Arctic Command*. Toronto: Ryerson Press, 1955.

Wise, Terence. *Polar Exploration*. London: Almark Publishing, 1973.

Young, Delbert A. *Last Voyage of the Unicorn*. Toronto: Clarke, Irwin, 1969.

Index

Acknowledgements

My thanks to Lesley Reynolds, former editor for the *Amazing Stories* series, for recommending this project to the Heritage Group publisher, Rodger Touchie, and to Rodger for agreeing that I should write this book.

In Canada, thanks to the ongoing support of long-time pal Steve Crowhurst and to my many friends in the great community of writers this country has produced. Across the Atlantic, a special thanks to the Swanwick Writers' Summer School in Derbyshire, England, for introducing me to a wonderful group of British writers in the late 1990s, especially Jill Butcher, the late Deric Longden, and Ray Allen. The friendship and support of my fellow writers in Canada, the US, and England over the years has been wonderful.

I (and many other nautical historians) am indebted to the New Netherland Museum and Half Moon Visitor's Center in Albany, New York, for republishing Robert Juet's journal from his 1609 expeditionary voyage with Henry Hudson, and for maintaining the *Half Moon* replica. Also, many thanks to the dedicated librarians in the Special Collections section of the Vancouver Public Library. And, for sheer depth of information, thanks to Ontario writer and historian Ian Chadwick for an excellent website on Henry Hudson.

Thanks again to my late uncle, Percy W. Corby, for introducing me to the tidal waters of the historic and highly commercial Thames River when I was a boy. Thanks also to my friend Roger MacAfee for keeping me humble on our large bookselling display at the annual Vancouver International Boat Show. Most important of all—thanks so much to all those readers from so many countries who have purchased my books and still keep coming back for more: without your support, none of this would be possible.

South Franklin St.
turn left.
"Eagle + Raven"

State Capitol Building.
State library.
Russian Orthodox church.
The Alaska Hotel. - Gold Rush.
Coffee

Red Dog Saloon.

"If we are not up to your standard
- lower them!"

Mendenhall Visitor Centre. Glaciers
Glacier Gardens - hummingbirds (tour or taxi)
Whale Watching.

SKAGWAY
8 Klondike Gold Rush - National Park.
700 people. Yellow building Tourist Centre, Park.
Train journey - book with Cruise
Golden Red Onion Saloon.
Arctic Brotherhood Hall. 800 pieces of driftwood
- tourist info for Skagway
Yellow bus tour
Yukon Rail - White Pass - amazing ride 3½ hrs.
Garden City of Alaska - rhubarb. Jewell Gardens
Chilkoot Trail - 3-5 days cafe - V. good

Glacier Bay | Sunday. "Men & Salmon came upstream to Spawn"
6:30 – 3.30 In crows nest. Talk about Glacier Bay

Ketchikan 10.30 – 5.30 – were bordellos. Airport.
Salmon capital of world. Pulp factory closed
Old cannery
Dolly's House Museum.
S.E. Alaska Discovery Museum
Tongass Historical Museum
Saxman Village
Lumberjack Show

Totem Right State Historical Center

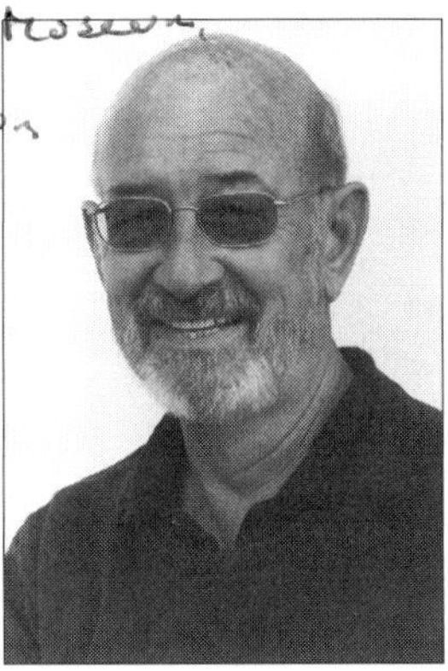

About the Author

Anthony Dalton is the author of thirteen non-fiction books and co-author of two others, many of which are about the sea, ships, and boats. These include *The Graveyard of the Pacific*; *A Long, Dangerous Coastline*; *The Fur-Trade Fleet*; *Fire Canoes*; *Baychimo: Arctic Ghost Ship*; *Alone Against the Arctic*; *Polar Bears*; and *Sir John Franklin*, all published by Heritage House. In addition, he wrote the foreword to Sir Robert McClure's *The Discovery of a Northwest Passage*, published by TouchWood Editions. His first novel, an ecological thriller about Royal Bengal tigers, was published in September 2013. Anthony is a Fellow of the Royal Geographical Society, a Fellow of the Royal Canadian Geographical Society, and past president of the Canadian Authors Association. He now spends much of each year at sea as a guest speaker for two cruise lines. When at home, he divides his time between Tsawwassen, BC, and the Gulf Islands.

Charda.
Fudge Factory

More Amazing Stories by Anthony Dalton

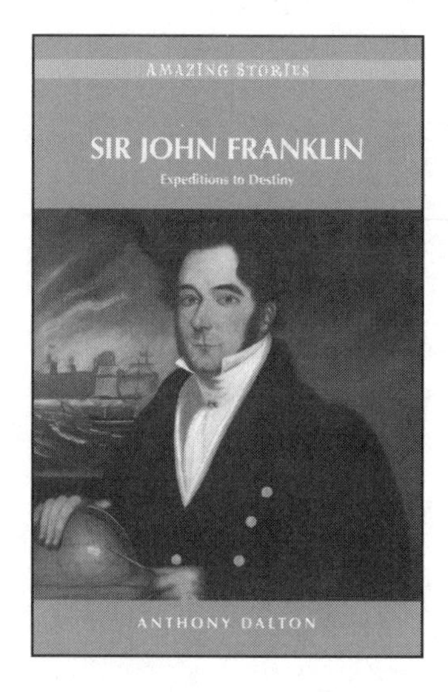

Sir John Franklin

Expeditions to Destiny

print ISBN 978-1-927051-81-8
ebook ISBN 978-1-927051-82-5

After Royal Navy captain Sir John Franklin disappeared in the Arctic in 1846, the search for his two ships and survivors of his expedition became one of the most exhaustive quests of the 19th century. Despite tantalizing clues, the ships were never found, and the fate of Franklin's expedition passed into legend as one of the North's great and enduring mysteries. Anthony Dalton explores the life of this fascinating man and retraces the route of the lost ships, recounting the sad tale of Franklin, his officers, and men in their final agonizing months.

Visit heritagehouse.ca to see the entire list of books in this series.

More Amazing Stories by Anthony Dalton

Fire Canoes

Steamboats on Great Canadian Rivers

print ISBN 978-1-927051-45-0
ebook ISBN 978-1-927051-46-7

Belching hot sparks, the first steamboat on the Canadian prairies was called a "fire canoe" by the local Cree. For 150 years, steamboats carried passengers and freight on great Canadian rivers. Travel back in time aboard goldrush paddle-steamers, rugged sternwheelers, and luxurious liners to the decades when steamboats sent the echoes of their shrill whistles across this land.

The Fur-Trade Fleet

Shipwrecks of the Hudson's Bay Company

print ISBN 978-1-926936-09-3
ebook ISBN 978-1-926936-07-9

Since the 17th century, hundreds of ships have sailed in the Hudson's Bay Company's fur-trade fleet, servicing far-flung northern posts and braving the wild rapids of mighty rivers. During these arduous voyages, many of these ships and their courageous crews came to grief. Here are the dramatic stories of the legendary ships that proudly flew the flag of Canada's oldest company.

Visit heritagehouse.ca to see the entire list of books in this series.

More Amazing Stories by Anthony Dalton

Polar Bears

The Arctic's Fearless Great Wanderers

print ISBN 978-1-926613-74-1
ebook ISBN 978-1-926936-25-3

Polar bears have become a charismatic symbol of animals threatened by climate change, yet in the past they were feared and hunted indiscriminately by Arctic adventurers. These fascinating stories draw from the annals of northern exploration and more recent polar bear research to capture the power and majesty of the world's largest land carnivore.

A Long, Dangerous Coastline

Shipwreck Tales from Alaska to California

print ISBN 978-1-926613-73-4
ebook ISBN 978-1-926936-11-6

From San Francisco's Golden Gate to the Inside Passage of British Columbia and Alaska, the west coast of North America has taken a deadly toll. Here are the dramatic tales of ships that met their end on this treacherous coastline—including *Princess Sophia*, *Queen of the North*, and others—and the tragic stories of those who sailed aboard them.